Parenting Education in Indonesia

A WORLD BANK STUDY

Parenting Education in Indonesia

Review and Recommendations to Strengthen Programs and Systems

Heather Biggar Tomlinson and Syifa Andina

WORLD BANK GROUP

Contents

Maps

Tables

About the Authors

Heather Biggar Tomlinson is an early childhood development specialist with 20 years of experience working in research, policy, and education sectors. She holds a PhD in developmental psychology. Heather has been a consultant for the World Bank and the United Nations Children's Fund an Association for the Advancement of Science Diplomacy Fellow in the office of Senator Edward Kennedy, a professional development specialist for the U.S. National Association for the Education of Young Children, and a research analyst for the National Institute of Child Health and Human Development. She is a coauthor of *The Early Years Matter: Education, Care, and the Well-Being of Children, Birth to 8* (2014), several chapters in the National Association for the Education of Young Children's flagship Developmentally Appropriate Practice series, and more than 20 other articles and reports. She recently co-developed award-winning parenting education modules for a government of Indonesia/World Bank program and currently runs a learning center for refugees in Jakarta.

Syifa Andina has been working in the field of early childhood care and development for almost 10 years. She has vast experiences in designing and delivering training, strategic planning, monitoring and evaluation, and development of modules, guidelines, and policies in Cambodia, Indonesia, and Timor Leste. Her areas of expertise are early childhood care and development, parenting education, community-based and child-centered approaches, and psychosocial supports for young children in emergency. She is the founder of the coalition of 28 civil society organizations across Indonesia with the focus of strengthening policy advocacy related to early childhood care and development, and the writer of the parenting education module for *Program Keluarga Harapan*, a countrywide program lead by the Ministry of Social Affairs reaching around 3 millions low-income households across Indonesia. She has worked for the World Bank, the United Nations Children's Fund, Plan International, World Vision, Save the Children, and the Ministry of Education of the government of Indonesia, and manages funding from various donors including AusAID and the American Red Cross.

Executive Summary

Introduction

Parenting education is important because parents have the most direct and powerful influence on children's well-being—more than teachers or friends. The term *parents* here refers to caregivers who provide primary care of children, whether biological parents, adoptive parents, grandparents, or other extended family or friends—those adults who protect, provide for, and nurture children so they can be well and succeed in life.

Yet, parents are not alone in having responsibility for children. Countries and communities also play important roles, as per the 2013 decree on early childhood development issued by the president of Indonesia and statements from the United Nations and others. In recognition of the humanitarian mandate and economic wisdom of investing in families with young children, the government of Indonesia aims to strengthen its existing parenting education system.

Little research exists on contemporary parenting styles and child outcomes in Indonesia. A 2013 World Bank impact evaluation found positive correlations between higher levels of parenting knowledge and abilities and better outcomes for children, beyond parents' income and education: Parents with higher levels of warmth and consistency, and lower levels of hostility, generally had children with fewer behavior problems, better health, increased emotional maturity, higher communication skills, and strong cognitive development (Hasan, Hyson, and Chang 2013). There is little other research, however, that identifies types of parenting styles in use in different regions or for different groups of families, or their related outcomes for children or communities.

In an effort to better understand and improve parenting education, the government of Indonesia commissioned a review of its existing programs to discover which programs have been implemented with which types of families and whether they are working to improve parents' knowledge and behaviors or child outcomes. This document summarizes the findings and recommendations of a review of current parenting education programs in Indonesia, analyses of published reports, interviews with ministry and nongovernmental organization (NGO) personnel, evaluation results, and field visits from 2013 to 2014. The focus of this review was on parenting education targeted at parents and caregivers of young children from birth to age eight years.

Programs Operating across the Archipelago

Four government ministries are currently involved in parenting education:

1. The Ministry of Health runs the *Kelas Ibu* (Mother Class) program for pregnant women and mothers of children younger than five years old.
2. The National Board on Family Planning (BKKBN) runs the *Bina Keluarga Balita* (BKB) program for parents of children from birth to age six years, often in coordination with early childhood education programs.
3. The Ministry of Social Affairs operates two programs, *Taman Anak Sejahtera* (TAS) and *Program Keluarga Harapan/*Family Development Sessions (PKH/ FDS), for families in poverty.
4. The Ministry of Education and Culture has two new grant initiatives, one for parents of children from birth to age six years, and the other for parents of infants and toddlers (from birth to age three years). In January 2015, it also established a Directorate for Parenting Education with the aim of increasing its efforts to improve parent involvement in education.

International NGOs also play an important role in supporting parenting education programs, including Plan Indonesia, which runs parenting groups such as *Kelompok Pengasuhan Anak* (KPA); Save the Children, which offers several programs (variously called BLEND, BISA, SPECIAL, BELAJAR, and SETARA); and World Vision, which offers parenting education through *Wahana Pendidikan Anak Usia Emas* (Vehicle for the Golden Period of Early Education).

Program providers most often offer classes for one to two hours once per month to groups of 15–35 parents. Many programs target poor families or families in poor areas. Data collection frequently occurs at district or provincial levels without being evaluated at the national level, so it is not known exactly how many families or which families are being served. Although each province offers at least three programs (through the Ministry of Health, Ministry of Education and Culture, and BKKBN), it is not known whether the same families receive multiple types of services and some families receive none because there is no coordination effort as yet.

Programs typically serve only a few dozen people at a time. As such, it can be said, with a fair degree of certainty, that the vast majority of families are not likely to receive all the relevant parenting education services that would benefit them at a period when the information is needed most. For example, a mother may receive one or two health sessions at a *posyandu* while pregnant but receives no further sessions related to health, education, positive discipline techniques, and play and interaction techniques during the child's formative years. Thus, although map ES.1 shows that there are at least a few programs in each province, it is important to note that some programs may serve only a handful of people in an area in which thousands or millions of people live.

Map ES.1 Parenting Education Program Coverage in Indonesia

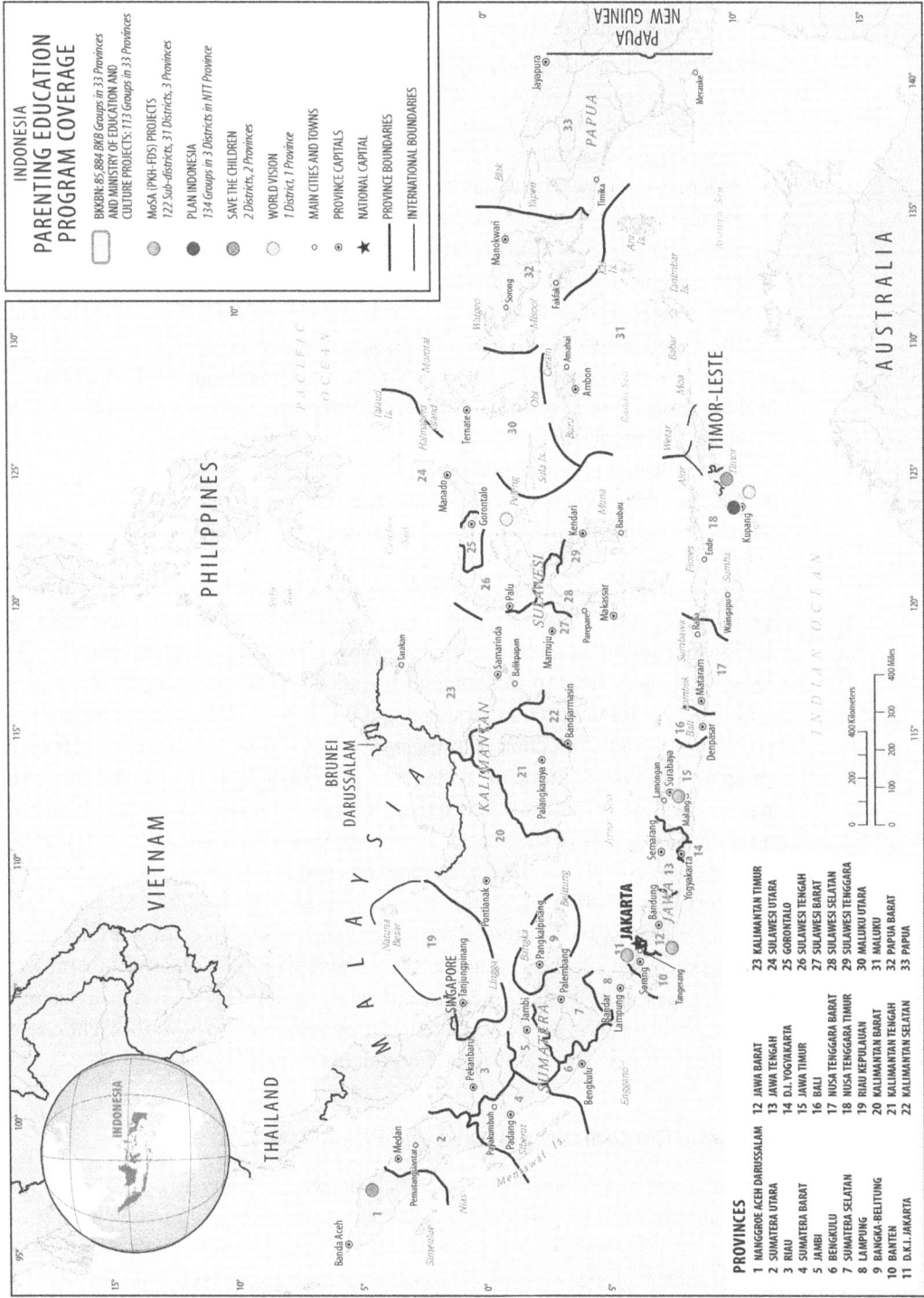

INDONESIA
PARENTING EDUCATION
PROGRAM COVERAGE

BKKBN: 85,884 BKB Groups in 33 Provinces
AND MINISTRY OF EDUCATION AND
CULTURE PROJECTS: 113 Groups in 33 Provinces

MoSA (PKH-FDS) PROJECTS
122 Sub-districts, 31 Districts, 3 Provinces

PLAN INDONESIA
134 Groups in 3 Districts in NTT Province

SAVE THE CHILDREN
2 Districts, 2 Provinces

WORLD VISION
1 District, 1 Province

○ MAIN CITIES AND TOWNS

⊙ PROVINCE CAPITALS

★ NATIONAL CAPITAL

— PROVINCE BOUNDARIES

— INTERNATIONAL BOUNDARIES

THAILAND

VIETNAM

PHILIPPINES

MALAYSIA

BRUNEI DARUSSALAM

SINGAPORE

PACIFIC OCEAN

INDIAN OCEAN

AUSTRALIA

PAPUA NEW GUINEA

PAPUA

TIMOR-LESTE

SUMATERA

KALIMANTAN

SULAWESI

JAWA

JAKARTA

Banda Aceh, Medan, Pematangsiantar, Pekanbaru, Padang, Jambi, Palembang, Bengkulu, Bandar Lampung, Tanjungpinang, Pangkalpinang, Pontianak, Palangkaraya, Banjarmasin, Samarinda, Balikpapan, Tarakan, Bandung, Semarang, Yogyakarta, Surabaya, Malang, Lamongan, Denpasar, Mataram, Mamuju, Makassar, Parepare, Palu, Kendari, Baubau, Gorontalo, Manado, Ternate, Ambon, Waingapu, Ende, Kupang, Manokwari, Sorong, Fakfak, Amahai, Biak, Timika, Jayapura, Merauke, Sewon, Tangerang

PROVINCES

1 NANGGROE ACEH DARUSSALAM
2 SUMATERA UTARA
3 RIAU
4 SUMATERA BARAT
5 JAMBI
6 BENGKULU
7 SUMATERA SELATAN
8 LAMPUNG
9 BANGKA-BELITUNG
10 BANTEN
11 D.K.I. JAKARTA
12 JAWA BARAT
13 JAWA TENGAH
14 D.I. YOGYAKARTA
15 JAWA TIMUR
16 BALI
17 NUSA TENGGARA BARAT
18 NUSA TENGGARA TIMUR
19 RIAU KEPULAUAN
20 KALIMANTAN BARAT
21 KALIMANTAN TENGAH
22 KALIMANTAN SELATAN
23 KALIMANTAN TIMUR
24 SULAWESI UTARA
25 GORONTALO
26 SULAWESI TENGAH
27 SULAWESI BARAT
28 SULAWESI SELATAN
29 SULAWESI TENGGARA
30 MALUKU UTARA
31 MALUKU
32 PAPUA BARAT
33 PAPUA

MARCH 2015

Box ES.1 Parenting Programs Work

Research from around the world shows that parenting education programs—when implemented well—are effective. Programs have been shown to do the following:

- Increase parents' sensitivity and nurturing behaviors
- Improve emotional abilities
- Reduce risks for low-birth weight babies
- Increase immunization rates, height, and weight
- Lead to greater safety at home and fewer clinic visits
- Replace violent discipline techniques with effective nonviolent ones
- Reduce rates of domestic abuse
- Lower rates of maternal depression, stress, and substance abuse
- Improve parents' capacity to appropriately interact with and stimulate their children
- Improve children's language and literacy skills; improve cognitive skills, school readiness, and academic achievement
- Reduce children's behavior problems
- Increase children's happiness and secure attachments to caregivers

---

Collectively, these programs reveal a dynamic and growing energy in Indonesia around parenting education programs. Regulations to consider early childhood holistically and in an integrated manner have taken root; program providers who have the leeway have moved beyond consideration for stunting, for example, to consideration for children's emotional and cognitive well-being as well. These are steps in the right direction. However, they are being taken at a program-by-program level at the moment, rather than at a national level, meaning that coverage by location or family characteristics is not yet systematic or need based. In addition, the quality of the programs seems to vary widely, and there is a consistent lack of data on both numbers of families reached and effectiveness of programs.

Effective parenting programs are those that help families use practices at home, such as implementing positive discipline techniques or stimulating language skills, that promote children's development in all areas in both the short run (for example, higher child compliance) and the long run (for example, higher graduation rates). To be effective, programs need to have the right content and the right delivery and design components (box ES.1).

Program Content: What Works and What Does Not

On the basis of a review of the materials of existing programs, many good messages are available for parenting programs for the general population of parents in Indonesia. What is lacking is intentionality in naming a selective set of messages that is meaningful to a given group of parents or aligned with ministry or community goals (for example, increasing enrollment in early childhood education programs, reducing the use of physical violence against children, reducing stunting and promoting healthy feeding practices, and raising language and cognitive scores in the early primary grades). Programs as presently run show one of two main errors: they tend to either provide no guidance to facilitators on what key messages to convey or provide too many key messages from which parents or facilitators are expected to choose. Instead, program providers should predetermine the focus of their programs, creating a relatively narrow and cohesive set of goals. Program providers should ensure that both facilitators and parents know what parents are expected to know and be able to do by the end of the program.

Well-articulated messages for particularly vulnerable families are also lacking. Families dealing with children with developmental delays or disabilities, chronic stress, illness, natural disasters, or conflict have special needs. Messages tailored to such families do not appear to be available as yet.

Examples of content areas could include learning about development and care in a child's first year; having positive interactions with children; improving emotional communication; teaching positive discipline techniques and behavior management; promoting children's social skills; or enhancing children's cognitive and academic skills. Parents in poor and otherwise vulnerable families would also benefit from a foundational awareness that parents are vital role models for their children regardless of how much money or education they have. They need better information about children's need for attention, conversation, affection, and stimulation from birth onward, and their innate drive to learn through play in early childhood. Increased awareness of the importance of early childhood education programs in fostering social and cognitive skills is also needed.

Program Design and Delivery: Strengths and Weaknesses

In addition to content, how providers organize and run their groups matters. Program design and delivery impact how well parents acquire new attitudes, knowledge, and skills. At the foundation, adult learning must occur actively with hands-on activities, interaction, reflection, and dialogue—as opposed to passively listening to facilitator lectures. In addition, research shows that good programs—those that result in lasting learning gains for parents—include the following components:

- *Active learning.* Learning occurs actively with hands-on activities, interaction, reflection, and dialogue, not passive listening alone. Facilitators use active learning approaches during sessions, such as participant discussion and practice with new skills.
- *Explicit goals.* Goals are explicitly stated as measurable outcomes.
- *Sufficient duration and intensity.* Programs are of sufficient length and intensity for the relevant population.
- *Practice.* There is in-session practice with children during some session time.
- *Appropriate content.* Programs coincide with developmental milestones or life transitions, such as an infant's first year of life, transition into an early childhood education or primary class, or in the aftermath of a trauma.

- *Responsiveness.* Programs are responsive to families' concrete needs.
- *Community support.* Planners have "buy-in" from the community.
- *Trained staff.* Program providers employ facilitators with appropriate skills and characteristics and support them with training, content and activity guidelines, supervision, and financial compensation.

There are several aspects of design and delivery programs that providers could improve to increase program effectiveness in Indonesia: (1) articulate goals with a specific audience in mind (do not try to be all things to all people); (2) ensure goals are measurable; (3) increase contact frequency and intensity; (4) include opportunity for in-session practice with children; (5) provide not only content guidelines but also step-by-step activity guidelines for facilitators; (6) improve selection processes, training, and compensation for facilitators; (7) use written forms to collect standardized data, review results, and make improvements; and (8) take better advantage of technology. Although these considerations hold true regardless of country, they are areas for improvement specific to contemporary programming in Indonesia in particular.

Recommended Next Steps for Improving the System

Given the preceding analysis, a recommended sequence of steps to strengthen the parenting education system in Indonesia is as follows (see table ES.1):

1. Relevant stakeholders at the national level come to consensus on which is the best agency to lead and coordinate parenting education programs, regardless of desired outcomes or delivery methods.
2. A list of the glaring gaps in knowledge about parenting in Indonesia is determined by scholars and academics. Initiatives to conduct research on parenting practices are implemented throughout Indonesia, with specific attention to regional differences and various types of vulnerable families, not only poor versus nonpoor.
3. The lead agency bolsters support for district-level agencies and together national and district offices conduct needs assessments throughout the districts to gather district-level information on parenting attitudes, knowledge, and skills. The data are compiled and analyzed at the national level.
4. Relevant stakeholders meet to finalize a list of goals at the national level that they would like to address through parenting education programs.
5. Parenting education program standards are established and agreed upon such that, regardless of desired outcomes or delivery methods, there is a quality benchmark each program should strive to achieve.
6. After determining the salient needs across districts, the lead agency identifies appropriate ministries or NGOs to design parenting education programs on specific topics and for specific audiences, either by using existing effective programs or by building new modules, making sure to create content and activity guidelines for facilitators.

7. Involved agencies hire and train a sufficient number of facilitators who have the relevant qualifications and characteristics to effectively implement the program. Facilitators receive both preservice and ongoing training using existing training agencies and institutions wherever possible, and provide an adequate compensation that goes beyond transportation reimbursement, to reduce turnover.

8. *Pemberdayaan Kesejahteraan Keluarga* (PKK), district offices, and the national lead agency work together to increase demand for parenting education programs among parents and communities, through public relations campaigns, parent outreach programs, and informational bulletins on social media.

9. Programs are implemented by the various responsible ministries and NGOs. Monitoring and evaluation (M&E) data inform continuous improvements to the programs, while the national lead agency provides feedback systems to all participating ministries and agencies and ensures targets are being met and no vulnerable families are going unserved.

10. An M&E agency independent of the lead agency is named and tasked with designing a system to capture baseline and regular follow-up data, analyzing results and making recommendations for improvements.

Table ES.1 Indonesia Parenting Education System: Matrix of Recommended Actions

Short-term (within 2 years)	Time (years)	Medium-term (3–5 years)	Time (years)
1. Develop the framework			
Reach consensus on lead agency that will provide oversight and coordination.	1	None	None
Develop and disseminate parenting education program standards.	1–2	None	None
Reach consensus on a discrete set of national goals for parenting education.	2	None	None
Task relevant ministries and NGOs with adapting or developing programs that align with district needs and national goals.	2	None	None
2. Create an enabling environment			
Leverage existing platforms of community engagement to incentivize experimentation at the community level to add or improve parenting education programs.	Initiate in year 1 and sustain	None	None
Increase demand for parenting education programs using public relations campaigns, parent outreach, and social media.	Initiate in year 1 and sustain	None	None

table continues next page

Table ES.1 **Indonesia Parenting Education System: Matrix of Recommended Actions** *(continued)*

Short-term (within 2 years)	Time (years)	Medium-term (3–5 years)	Time (years)
3. Conduct the research			
Conduct needs assessments at the district level on service delivery gaps for parenting education programs.	1	Reevaluate districts' needs as necessary.	3–5
Determine gaps in the knowledge base about parenting practices and outcomes within diverse cultural, socioeconomic, and disadvantaged groups in Indonesia; conduct studies to close these gaps and inform design of improved programs.	1–2	Continue the research programs.	3–5
Develop core materials for parenting education programs in light of research findings.	2	Pilot core materials.	3–4
Develop training procedure for facilitators of parenting education programs.	2	Pilot training for facilitators.	3–4
Engage M&E experts to inform the development of indicators and rigorous study designs to evaluate the effectiveness of these new parenting education programs.	Initiate in year 1 and sustain	Ensure M&E experts continue to participate in analyzing and using research results to refine program content and delivery.	3–5
4. Implement and refine programming			
Develop monitoring mechanisms to ensure data are compiled, analyzed, and used to make program improvements.	Initiate in year 1 and sustain	Refine parenting education programs on the basis of lessons from monitoring.	Initiate in year 3 and sustain
Train master trainers using existing training facilities and institutions.	2	Hire and train facilitators to implement the respective programs. Ensure continuous professional development opportunities for facilitators.	Initiate in year 3 and sustain
Plan expanded implementation strategies to ensure access to all target families.	2	Scale up effective programs to increase coverage and reach appropriate target families.	Initiate in year 4 and sustain
		Compare progress against national goals and revise strategies accordingly.	Initiate in year 4 and sustain

Note: M&E = monitoring and evaluation; NGO = nongovernmental organization.

Abbreviations

BELAJAR	Better Literacy for Academic Results
BISA	Basic Initiative for School Access
BKB	*Bina Keluarga Balita*
BKKBN	*Badan Kependudukan dan Keluarga Berencana Nasional* (National Board on Family Planning)
BLEND3	Better Living, Education, Nutrition and Development 3
CMECCD	Community-Managed Early Childhood Care and Development
ECD	Early Childhood Development
FDS	Family Development Session
HI-ECD	Holistic Integrated-Early Childhood Development
KKA	*Kartu Kemajuan Anak* (Child Development Chart)
KPA	*Kelompok Pengasuhan Anak*
M&E	monitoring and evaluation
MCHIP	Maternal and Child Health Integrated Program
MoEC	Ministry of Education and Culture
MoH	Ministry of Health
MoSA	Ministry of Social Affairs
NGO	nongovernmental organization
NTT	*Nusa Tenggara Timur*
PAUD	*Pendidikan Anak Usia Dini* (Early Childhood Education and Development)
PKH/FDS	*Program Keluarga Harapan*/Family Development Sessions
PKK	*Pemberdayaan Kesejahteraan Keluarga*
PKSA	*Program Kesejahteraan Sosial Anak*
RPJMN	*Rencana Pembangunan Jangka Menengah*
SETARA	Strengthening Education through Awareness and Reading Achievement
SPECIAL	Safe and Positive Education for Children in Indonesia with Active Learning

TAS	*Taman Anak Sejahtera*
UNESCO	United Nations Educational, Scientific, and Cultural Organization
UNICEF	United Nations Children's Fund
USAID	United States Agency for International Development

CHAPTER 1

Introduction

Abstract

Children need warmth, responsiveness, attention, conversation, consistency, and predictability from their parents and other caregivers. Parenting education programs are an excellent avenue to teach or remind parents to foster these attributes and activities and to use positive strategies to interact with children. They can encourage change in parents' attitudes and behaviors to better promote children's social skills, confidence, joy, and achievement in school and life.

However, such successes are not won easily. Program planning takes thoughtfulness, coordination among stakeholders, and adaptation for specific goals, family background, and cultural context. This can be a challenge in a country with the rich diversity of Indonesia. Both the Government of Indonesia and nongovernmental organizations (NGOs) have made in-roads to building good parenting education programs, but the network is not yet solid nor reaching all families. The aim of this report is to describe what programs exist, how they function, how well they function, and what can be done to strengthen individual programs and the system overall.

Parenting Education Matters Because Parents Matter

Parent programs broadly described aim to improve parents' and children's well-being by creating awareness of the importance of parents' role in supporting children's development and success and strengthening or modifying parents' attitudes, beliefs, or practices in caring for their child. These types of programs are variously called *parenting programs, parent education, parenting education programs, parent training, adult education,* and *parent support programs.* However, parenting as related to adults' skill in and capacity to care for their children, is only one category of content that a parenting program might include; others could be related to adult literacy education, workforce skills development, poverty reduction, and other general adult-education content. In this study, we use the term *parenting education* to emphasize our focus on parenting skills as they relate to the quality of care and interactions between parents and children.

Parenting education is important because parents, more than teachers, friends, or other caregivers, typically have the most direct and powerful influence on children's well-being. "While it is recognized that not all children are raised by their parents, nonetheless, all children require quality parenting," as UNESCO author Judith Evans (2006) noted. For optimal development, children need at least one invested, caring adult who cares about and values the child, a primary caregiver the child is close to and can count on and trust to provide for their physical, emotional, and developmental needs. Caring certainly means keeping a child safe and protected from harm, but that is not sufficient. Caring also means interacting with children so they stay in good physical and emotional health; have chances to listen and be listened to; experience physical and emotional affection; have opportunities to explore the world, be curious, and problem solve; and develop their physical skills, social-emotional abilities, language and cognitive skills, and moral capacities and spirituality with the guidance of someone who enjoys interacting with them. Recognizing that a variety of people within a family or community can be essential caregivers to children, the term *parent* in our study refers to mothers, fathers, grandmothers, or other caregivers who have a primary caregiving relationship with children.

Parents are not alone in having the responsibility to take of children. Countries and communities also play important roles, per the 1990 United Nations' Convention on the Rights of the Child and the 2013 decree on early childhood development by the President of Indonesia (President of the Republic of Indonesia 2013). In recognition of the humanitarian mandate and economic wisdom of investing in families with young children, the Government of Indonesia is looking for ways to strengthen its existing parenting education programs.

The government oversees parenting education programs through the Ministry of Health (MoH), the Ministry of Education and Culture (MoEC), the Ministry of Social Affairs (MoSA), and the National Board on Family Planning (*Badan Kependudukan dan Keluarga Berencana Nasional* or BKKBN). Several nongovernmental organizations also play a role in parenting education programs in Indonesia, such as Plan Indonesia, Save the Children, and World Vision. This study summarizes the programs overseen by these seven agencies.[1]

Even though they use different approaches, materials, training frameworks, and messages, all of these organizations use parenting education as a means to improving the lives of children across the country. While the goal of improving the lives of children is central, it is equally critical to consider parents not merely as a means to an end (that is, to support children), but as people deeply deserving of the country's attention in and of themselves. Parents are often vulnerable, unsure, and in need of help regardless of geography, education, or wealth—although the most disadvantaged populations are especially in need of help. Parents are worthy of the nation's financial investment, intellectual talent, and moral and emotional support simply because they will benefit and prosper from it themselves. As parents deepen relationships, gain confidence, and improve their knowledge and skills, they will enrich the lives of their children, empower their families, and improve their communities now and into the future.

Parenting Education in Indonesia • http://dx.doi.org/10.1596/978-1-4648-0621-6

Background and Overview of the Report

Background

Indonesia strongly promotes and upholds by decree the importance of a holistic and integrated approach to early childhood development, referred to as Holistic, Integrated Early Childhood Development (HI-ECD). That is, based on the research showing that children need to develop well across domains in order to thrive, several ministries provide services to improve child and family well-being in children's early years. Stakeholders in various fields including health, education, psychology, child protection, family welfare, parenting programs, community programs, and so forth, serve children and families and coordinate some aspects of service but not all. As a result, early childhood has many stakeholders—but not a clear champion. Indonesia is not alone in this conundrum; many countries have several stakeholders but no clear champion. In Indonesia, stakeholders have worked well together to build a respectable system of early childhood education services, in spite of the challenges. Challenges include less access to programs for children in poorer areas; lack of awareness among parents; and unqualified teachers, to name a few. Nonetheless, programs offered for young children such as playgroups, preschools (PAUD) and kindergartens (TK) have steadily risen in number and quality over the last decade due to government investments in early childhood education.

However, a system to provide programs for *parents* to improve their parenting skills and abilities to provide a steady, safe, and stimulating environment for their children is still in early days. Many of the same challenges apply to parenting education programs as to early childhood education programs: less service provision in poor areas, very few training and professional development opportunities for facilitators, low awareness and therefore low demand among parents, and financial constaints. Additional challenges include virtually no data collection on parenting education programs, no parenting education program standards exist, and no body has yet been given coordinating responsibilities for parenting education writ large—although MoEC in January 2015 is exploring the establishment of a Directorate General for Parenting Education related to improving children's educational success.

Each four years, the Government puts forth a planning document for ministry program goals, the *Rencana Pembangunan Jangka Menengah* (RPJMN). According to RPJMN 2015–19, released in January 2015, there are three goals related to parenting education under two ministries of the current administration, presented here with associated indicators and target growth from 2015 to 2019:

1. MoEC: More extensive and equal access to early childhood education and adult education on the basis of gender equality and sustainable development at province and district levels.
   a. Indicator: The number of centers providing parenting education should grow from 39,724 to 87,417.
   b. Indicator: The number of parents/caregivers who participate in parenting education should increase from 255,500 to 4,343,500.

2. MoEC: Parent/caregiver receives parenting education in order to improve their knowledge and understand how to educate children from the fetal stage into adulthood.
   a. Indicator: Number of school committees or parent associations implementing character building should grow from 10,000 to 20,000.
   b. Indicator: The number of nonformal education services providing character building and life skills, including nutrition knowledge, should grow from 5,000 to 10,000.
   c. Indicator: The number of education services providing character building and knowledge of domestic violence and child sexual harassment should increase from 5,000 to 10,000.
3. BKKBN: Increased knowledge, attitudes, and behavior of child growth and development.
   a. Indicator: The percentage of families with toddlers and children who understand and implement nurturing parenting in relation to child growth and development should increase from 50.2 percent to 70.5 percent.

These goals are a step in the right direction, although the two MoEC goals are input based (focused on number of programs) rather than outcome based (focused on changes in parents' and children's attitudes, knowledge, and well-being). The BKKBN goal is well phrased as an outcome, though more specific ways of measuring how well parents understand and implement nurturing parenting will be needed once data collection begins. These are some of outcome based goals specific to Indonesia that research suggests bear attention:

• Increased awareness of good feeding and nutrition practices in infancy and early childhood to reduce stunting
• Increased self-esteem among poor or less educated parents
• Increased awareness of the power of parents to impact children's self-esteem, achievement, and sense of well-being
• Heightened knowledge about the importance of parent engagement with infants, toddlers, and young children through conversation, attention, play, storytelling or reading, and other types of stimulation
• Knowledge about child safety in the home and supervision outside the home
• Increased awareness of the importance of sending children to preschool, and knowledge about what constitutes high-quality early childhood education, including having a balance of child-initiated activities (for example, free play) and teacher-initiated activities (for example, instruction)
• Increased demand for high-quality early childhood education
• Higher language and cognitive scores among children
• Reduced use of physical violence as a means of child discipline.

This is not an exhaustive list, but these are several of the outcomes agencies in Indonesia would do well to address.

Aims

This report aims to provide all relevant early childhood stakeholders with background information about extant parenting education programs in order that the stakeholders may better coordinate their coverage, sharpen the selection of key messages, and raise the quality of program implementation. Although parenting education is needed for parents of all ages of children, the current work focuses on children in the early years, from birth to about age eight years. The higher level outcomes one would hope to see as a result of this collection of information would be a stronger system of parenting education with improved coordination, implementation of parenting performance indicators and data collection across agencies, and eventually higher levels of parent and child well-being. Thus, the overarching goal of this study was to pull scattered information together in writing in a cohesive way in order that relevant ministries can decide together how best to build a unified system to replace the currect piecemeal approach which leaves many families out and leaves many facilitators without the support needed to do their job effectively.

Methods

The government of Indonesia commissioned The World Bank to complete a review of current parenting education programs in operation in the country in order to determine what exists, what works, and how to strengthen programs and the system overall. The authors solicited information from knowledgeable stakeholders in relevant organizations to discern which agencies have currently active or emerging programs. We then completed desk reviews of all materials we could gather related to each program and conducted interviews with government and NGO staff responsible for or involved with the relevant parenting education programs. We conducted field visits, attended relevant conferences, and listened to data presentations to gather information as well.

In some cases, we excluded ministries or organizations that may have related roles but are not directly responsible for programs (for example, Ministry of Women's Empowerment, United Nations Educational, Scientific, and Cultural Organization [UNESCO], United Nations Children's Fund [UNICEF]). In many cases, programs are emerging or changing rapidly (for example, *Program Keluarga Harapan*/Family Development Sessions [PKH/FDS], BKKBN), in which case we provide the latest information available while recognizing things may change between the time of writing and the time of reading this report. Data collection and analysis occurred primarily from September 2013 through March 2014. In all cases, we relied heavily on interview information and less on written documents, which frequently were not available.

Structure of the Report

Subsequent to this Introduction, the report is organized as follows. Chapter 2 provides a literature review on parenting education programs in general, based on findings from various countries. Although most research has occurred in developed countries, research from impoverished or otherwise marginalized groups in those countries offers insight into comparable groups in Indonesia. Moreover, there is relevant research from some developing countries that can inform Indonesia's plans. In chapter 3, we discuss what is known about parenting in Indonesia based on one empirical study and some qualitative information. In chapter 4, we summarize seven programs on the basis of their relevance as potential players in improving either the content or delivery mechanisms of parenting education programs in Indonesia: Government programs including the Ministry of Health's *Kelas Ibu* (Mother Class) program, the National Board on Family Planning's *Bina Keluarga Balita* (BKB) program, the Ministry of Social Affairs' two programs, *Taman Anak Sejahtera* (TAS) and *Program Keluarga Harapan*/Family Development Sessions (PKH/FDS), and the Ministry of Education and Culture's two new grant initiatives and new Directorate General of Parenting Education. In addition, we describe nongovernmental organization (NGO) programs including Plan Indonesia's parenting groups, *Kelompok Pengasuhan Anak* (KPA), Save the Children's programs (variously called BLEND, BISA, SPECIAL, BELAJAR, and SETARA), and World Vision's approach, *Wahana Pendidikan Anak Usia Emas* (Vehicle for the Golden Period of Early Education). Although programs vary in their approaches, materials, and messages, there are many commonalities in programs' strengths and weaknesses. Chapter 5 offers a discussion and recommendations in light of overall strengths and weaknesses across programs and the overall system of support for parents in Indonesia.

Note

1. UNICEF has supported both government and nongovernmental parenting education programs in Indonesia and supports BKKBN's systems, but currently does not operate its own program. UNESCO offers effective materials for disadvantaged parents in other countries in the Southeast Asia region, but stakeholders have not adapted them for use in Indonesia. Therefore the efforts of these two influential organizations are not discussed in this study.

CHAPTER 2

Literature Review on Parenting Education Internationally

Abstract

Many adults play an important role in caring for, encouraging, protecting, and teaching young children: Child care providers and teachers can be important caregivers and early role models, religious leaders and coaches often have a lasting impact, and grandparents and extended family members frequently play a central role in children's lives. Yet, the most powerful influence on children's sense of love, security, guidance, and success is unequivocally parents.

Components of Parenting

Parents influence children in several major ways. The following is one approach researchers have used to describe and evaluate parenting as it occurs beyond providing food and shelter (Brooks-Gunn and Markman 2005):

1. *Nurturance*—ways of expressing love, affection, and care, being warm and sensitive to changes in children's behaviors, and having low levels of detachment, intrusiveness, and negative regard.
2. *Discipline*—responses to children's behavior that parents deem appropriate or inappropriate based on child gender, age, parental beliefs, upbringing, and culture.
3. *Teaching*—conveying information or skills to children through activities, discussion, questions, modeling, and opportunities for practice and experiences.
4. *Language*—communication between parents and children that conveys knowledge, emotion, values, and culture and is measured by number of words heard, length of sentences, questions asked, elaborations on child speech, events discussed, storytelling, and presence and style of reading activities.
5. *Materials*—the number and use of cognitively and linguistically stimulating materials parents provide to children in the home, which can overlap with language and teaching activities, and is often associated with family income.

6. *Monitoring*—watchfulness and supervision of children's safety and well-being, such as periodically checking on a child who is playing alone, observing what a child sees during screen time, and knowing who the child is with and what the child is doing when not at home.

7. *Management*—scheduling events, carrying out planned events, whether that means going to a playground or getting immunization shots, and overseeing the rhythm of the household, such as bedtime and mealtime routines, all of which often takes a great deal of parenting time and energy.

Can these and other components of parenting be changed and improved—do parenting interventions work? Research shows that when programs are implemented well, they have positive impacts on a range of child and family outcomes. The key caveat is *when implemented well*.

Evidence That Parenting Programs Work When Implemented Well

Research from the past two decades guides us to limit our expectations for parenting education programs if they are not implemented well—that is, by knowledgeable, supportive facilitators, occurring with the right degree of intensity and contact hours, and at the right time to meet parents' needs. If programs are not implemented well, are infrequent, lacking intensity and follow-up, not contextually relevant, and not individualized for children's specific ages and family's needs, they are likely to have little to no impact. Parents are not likely to change their attitudes and behaviors—especially disadvantaged parents (Chilman 1973; Hoff-Ginsberg and Tardif 1995; Howrigan 1988).

On the other hand, parenting education programs have repeatedly proven effective for parents of young children in both developed and developing countries when delivered well. They can in fact be *most* effective with the neediest families, including in low- and middle-income countries (Eshel et al. 2006; Evans 2006). Parenting interventions in developed and developing countries, whether through home visiting programs, group sessions, or some combination of approaches, have been shown to correlate with the following positive outcomes:

• Increase parents' sensitivity to their children, reduce negativity towards children, improve parents' emotional abilities, expressiveness, responsiveness and sensitivity in interactions and nurturing behaviors, help parents be less intrusive and better able to support children's independence (Brooks-Gunn, Berlin, and Fuligni 2000; Cooper et al. 2002; Heinicke et al. 2001; Olds et al. 2004).

• Reduce subsequent pregnancies for at-risk parents (Kitzman et al. 1997), reduce low-birth weight babies for expectant mothers (Lee et al. 2009), and improve health outcomes for low birth weight babies, including eliminating expected developmental delays (Brooks-Gunn et al. 1994; Walkeret al. 2004).

- Increase immunization rates, child nutrition levels, and child height and weight (Cooper et al. 2002; Johnson, Howell, and Molloy 1993; Super, Herrera, and Mora 1990).
- Lead to greater safety maintenance at home (Bugental and Schwartz 2009) and fewer clinic visits for accidents and injuries (Kitzman et al. 1997).
- Reduce domestic abuse and replace violent discipline techniques with effective nonphysical approaches (Barlow et al. 2006; Bugental and Schwartz 2009; Duggan et al. 1999; Webster-Stratton and Reid 2010). Researchers suggest that parenting interventions are instrumental in preventing child maltreatment in low- and middle-income countries (Knerr, Gardner, and Cluver 2013).
- Reduce mothers' depressive symptoms and substance abuse and reduce parents' stress levels (Administration for Children and Families [AFC] 2002; Black et al. 1994; Duggan et al. 1999; Gelfand et al. 1996; Love et al. 2005).
- Improve parents' verbal responsiveness to children, provide more stimulating activities to children, increase parents' level of reading to children, strengthen children's language and literacy skills, increase children's problem-solving skills, improve school readiness, cognitive skills and academic achievement, and narrow achievement gaps between majority and minority group children (Black et al. 1994; Brooks-Gunn and Markman 2005; Johnson, Howell, and Molloy 1993; Landry et al. 2012; Myers and Hertenberg 1987; Reese, Sparks, and Leyva 2010; Turner, Nye, and Schwartz 2004/2005; Gardner et al. 2003).
- Reduce children's behavioral problems and improve children's behavior and cooperativeness (Centers for Disease Control and Prevention 2009; Gardner et al. 2003).
- Increase children's emotional abilities, happiness, and rates of children's secure attachments with caregivers (Gardner et al. 2003; Heinicke et al. 1999; Jacobson and Frye 1991; Van den Boom 1995).

These studies and a multitude of others collectively underscore the relevance of parenting education programs as an avenue to instigating changes in values and behavior that centrally impact children but ripple outwards to impact communities, schools, and society. What is it that good programs teach to bring about these positive changes, and how do they teach effectively? We discuss these two questions next.

Content of Parenting Education Programs

First we review results about the "what" of parenting education, or the content about which parents learn; then we follow with the "how," which is design and delivery.

Common Content Components

The U.S. Centers for Disease Control and Prevention (CDC 2009) conducted a meta-analysis of 77 studies on parent training for parents of children from birth to age seven years. The CDC researchers analyzed several content components of the programs included in the meta-analysis. Any given program may have provided all of these components or a combination of some of them but not all—and it should be noted that programs should not include *all* of these content areas, but rather should select content that aligns with community needs and program goals. Results for the CDC meta-analysis were evaluated in light of which components appeared to work well consistently across all programs to improve parenting skills and reduce children's problem behaviors, two out of many possible goals.

- Knowledge of Child Development and Care. Content on child development might include teaching new parents about feeding, home safety and supervision of children, developmental milestones, typical behaviors at various ages, and providing stimulating environments (CDC 2009).
- Positive Interactions with Children. This type of content focuses on the importance of positive interactions between parents and children, such as providing positive attention and physical affection, spending time together, communicating well, and offering appropriate recreational activities—activities not related to disciplining a child. Parents learn to respond sensitively to children's emotional and psychological needs, to soothe children and nurture them, and to encourage children to play and be creative (CDC 2009; Huser, Small, and Eastman 2008).
- Emotional Communication. This component is linked to but not exactly the same as positive interactions with children. Parents learn how to help children identify their own emotions and appropriately express them, a precursor to recognizing emotions in others and developing empathy. Parents may need to learn to reduce criticisms of their children and sarcasm, instead elevating their respect for their children and allowing children to feel like important contributors to the communication process. It is a key relationship-building skill that is critical for the success of other parenting skills (CDC 2009).
- Discipline and Behavior Management. Managing children's misbehavior is not easy in the best of circumstances and is highly challenging for parents with few resources and high stress levels. Content on discipline starts with teaching parents good disciplinary communication, such as giving clear and age-appropriate directions, setting rules and limits, and stating expectations and consequences in advance of misbehavior. Specific topics further include: attitudes about discipline strategies; attributions about children's misbehavior; monitoring and supervising children; specific reinforcement and consequences, such as planned ignoring, positive reinforcement, and time out; problem solving about child behaviors; and consistency in responding to misbehaviors (CDC 2009; Huser, Small, and Eastman 2008).
- Promoting Children's Social Skills and Prosocial Behavior. Parents learn to teach children to share, use good manners, get along with other children, and cooperate (CDC 2009).
- Promoting Children's Cognitive and Academic Skills. This content typically teaches parents how to improve children's school readiness and foster language and literacy skills.

Effective Components for Improving Parenting Skills and Child Behavior

Of these various content components, researchers found four components show-ing the largest effect sizes for the following four components (that is, programs including these components showed greater improvements in terms of better parenting skills for parents and better behavior for children than programs with-out these components):

1. *Emotional communication skills*—focusing on this improved parents' parenting skills and behaviors
2. *Positive parent–child interaction skills*—focusing on positive interactions led to better results for parents *and* children
3. *Teaching parents how to correctly use time out* as a discipline strategy benefited children
4. *Teaching parents to be consistent* in responding to their children was associated with better child behavior.

These results suggest the health and strength of the parent-child relationship—based on warm and caring interactions, good communication, and positive, con-sistent discipline—is at the heart of family's well-being. Adding or enhancing the four aforementioned elements would be useful for programs aiming to improve parenting skills and children's behavior, though other components may effec-tively address other outcomes, such as children's cognition and success in school.

Design and Delivery Components of Successful Programs

Program delivery mechanisms—the "how" of parenting education—also matters. In successful programs, the following things occur.

Program Goals Are Explicitly Stated as Measurable Outcomes

Programs that name and evaluate very specific outcome goals are more likely to impact attitudinal and behavioral changes among parents (Colosi and Dunifon 2003). Naming targeted outcomes (for example, to increase fathers' participation in parenting, to increase the percentage of children living above the poverty line, to decrease the incidence of abuse) and designing programs with evaluation of those outcomes in mind is critical to seeing results. By extension, following through on the planned evaluations, whether through experimental or quasi-experimental designs, is central to effective programs.

Programs Are of Sufficient Length and Intensity

How long a program lasts and how often parents should meet depends on the target population of parents. Poor or otherwise vulnerable parents are likely to need at least 30–40 contact hours between themselves and teachers/facilitators for positive impacts. Moreover, they need multiple contacts each week, such as through class, home visits, newsletters, phone calls or messages, and so forth

(Huser, Small, and Eastman 2008; Kumpfer 1999). Many programs with high-risk families fail because they are too short to produce behavior changes and increase protective factors within the family. In addition, high-risk parents often miss sessions or have trouble knowing how to implement new skills on their own at home. Studies by Powell and Grantham-McGregor (cited in Malhomes and King 2012) with poor and urban children in Jamaica compared the effects on children related to how often parents received support, in this case in the form of home visits. Children of parents receiving a home visit once per month showed negligible changes in their developmental progress after one year, compared to control-group children. Children of parents visited every fortnight showed modest progress. Children of parents who met once per week showed the most progress in terms of degree of development and the number of areas of development affected. Programs that occur over at least one year are likely to see sustained behavior changes, and programs lasting two to three years are even more likely to correlate with changes (Evans 2006).

On the other hand, programs that are too long are likely to lose busy parents, especially those parents experiencing no problems or only minor problems with their children. Interventions with low-risk families require less contact time (Colosi and Dunifon 2003). Researchers recommend that once a program has been created and field tested for effectiveness, implementers should adhere to the predetermined implementation timeline and should not try to condense the material or squeeze the timeline into a shorter duration (Huser, Small, and Eastman 2008).

Active Learning
A critical component to consider is whether a program requires parents to *actively* acquire information and skills through activities such as homework, modeling, and practicing skills—in contrast to merely receiving information through passive listening. Decades of research show that active learning approaches are more effective than passive approaches (Arthur et al. 1998; Grindal et al. 2013; Joyce and Showers 2002; Salas and Cannon-Bowers 2001). In the CDC meta-analysis (2009), the authors excluded programs that only provided information passively (that is, through lectures and videos alone) because they lacked the necessary active acquisition of information required for successful outcomes. All 77 studies included used active learning components that encouraged or required parents' participation in the learning process, whether through reflection and dialogue, role playing, simulation, homework, in-session interactions with children, and so forth. The researchers' categorical exclusion of programs based on passive approaches to learning underscores the critical need to ensure that programs are interactive, participatory, and based on parents' active learning.

In-Session Practice with Children
Results from the CDC meta-analysis (2009) showed that in a comparison of six delivery components evaluated,[1] one was especially important for improving

parents' *and* children's behaviors: Requiring parents to practice with their child during sessions, a concept referred to in Indonesian as *pengasuhan bersama*. The immediate reinforcement and corrective feedback was a critical link to solidifying parents' mastery of new skills. This was found not only in the CDC meta-analysis, but in other reviews by Grindal et al. (2013), Huser, Small, and Eastman (2008), and Colosi and Dunifon (2003), all of which noted that programs should target a family rather than an individual, as families work in systems. Family programs may include parent skills training, children's social skills development, a focus on parent-child interactions, and activities to strengthen parent-child relationships. Not all participants need to be present at all times, but at some points in the overall program, observing parents and children together is beneficial. These findings are consistent with the literature in education that shows that learning is most effective when it occurs in ways that are meaningful within participants' life context and natural environments. In sum, the programs from which parents most consistently benefited, according to CDC (2009), were those with an in-session opportunity for parent-child interaction to practice new skills.

Programs Coincide with Developmental Milestones or Life Transitions

The most effective programs take advantage of teachable moments—developmental change phases among children that may bewilder or frustrate parents—and natural transitions (Colosi and Dunifon 2003; Huser, Small, and Eastman 2008). These are the times when parents have questions and benefit most from knowledgeable resources. For example, programs focusing on the post-natal period and the first year of life offer crucial support for new parents, or programs designed to help children begin at an ECD program or transition into primary school are ideal opportunities for providing input when parents need it.

Programs Are Responsive to Families' Concrete Needs

Successful programs occur at times and in locations that are appropriate to families' needs, rather than at the convenience of facilitators, program implementers, or facility managers. Program planners anticipate and provide for basic needs when possible, such as meals and child care (Huser, Small, and Eastman 2008).

Programs Have "Buy-in" from the Community

Programs tend to be most successful in changing behaviors when multiple stakeholders within a community agree with and explicitly support the content and delivery of the program (Kumpfer 1999). Program designers collaborate with school officials, local groups and community organizations, religious leaders, and local government agencies or administrators who can reinforce the messages families hear. It is helpful to ensure consistency between home and school. Delivering the programs at public sites such as schools or in community centers may increase the success of programs as well (Colosi and Dunifon 2003), although this is not a requirement for successful programs and would depend on the goals and logistical paramaters of the community. The key is that officials, business owners, schools, religious leaders, and citizens in the community understand and agree with the need for parent services.

Programs Employ Facilitators with Certain Knowledge, Skills, and Characteristics

Successful programs do not merely use whoever volunteers to help out as a facilitator; rather, program owners select professionals or paraprofessionals with relevant knowledge of child development and care and skills related to adult learning. Sessions tend to be most effective when facilitators have certain character traits. It is helpful to have facilitators with whom participants can relate—they may reflect the demographic make-up of participants in terms of ethnicity, religion, and language. More important, however, are personal characteristics, especially respect and appreciation for parents and all they do or are trying to do—they respect parents' values, aim to strengthen parental authority in positive ways, and focus on families' strengths rather than trying only to fix apparent weaknesses. In addition, qualities such as warmth, genuineness, flexibility, humor, empathy, communication skills, willingness to share, and sensitivity to group processes associate with good outcomes. In addition, credibility and experience with children matters (Huser, Small, and Eastman 2008).

Beyond selecting facilitators based on articulated criteria and characteristics, program owners with successful programs support facilitators. They teach them relevant knowledge and skills through adequate training that occurs both before programs begin (preservice training) and provide ongoing support as programs continue (in-service training). They ensure that facilitators have strong guidance on key messages and pedagogy by providing clear guidelines or curricula that cover both content and activities. The provide support from more experienced professionals through mentoring, coaching, or supervision so that facilitators benefit from feedback and advice (Wasik and Bryant 2009). And they treat facilitators as the professionals they are by paying them a reasonable incentive or salary that goes beyond transportation reimbursements (Whitebook and Eichberg n.d.). Investing financially creates a sustainable workforce and reduces the facilitator turnover that increases hiring and training costs, diminishes the knowledge base among facilitators, and robs programs and facilitators of parent and community trust and respect.

In summary, the literature is clear that parenting education programs can work very effectively to increase parents' awareness and capacities to provide good parenting to their children and to improve children's lives, especially for the neediest families. However, to be effective, programs need to have certain content and delivery components in place, and they need to be relevant and meaningful within families' cultural and environmental contexts. In chapter 3, we discuss some of the issues relevant to parenting within various contexts in Indonesia.

Note

1. The six components evaluated included (1) using guidelines or other curriculum materials, (2) modeling, (3) requiring homework, (4) rehearsal, role playing, or in-session practice, (5) providing separate child instruction, and (6) including ancillary services.

Parenting in Indonesia

Abstract

Indonesia includes a wide and complex array of cultures, ethnicities, languages, and geography. The diversity makes for a dynamic and culturally rich nation, but one that is challenging to characterize with any simplicity. In some areas of research, it is challenging to characterize even with caveats because virtually no research has been done, and parenting is one of those areas. As Chao and Tseng (2002) noted in their review of Asian parenting, Indonesia has rarely been included in studies of parenting. It is likely that Indonesian parents use a wide variety of parenting styles. The authors noted that there are "greater difficulties in identifying unified cultural principles in these countries that have vast regional or island differences and that have been influenced by extensive colonization," both of which describe Indonesia (p. 65). Researchers at the World Health Organization also have noted that while Indonesia is one of several developing countries that offers parenting interventions, there is a lack of published studies tracking outcomes for those interventions (Eshel et al. 2006).

The Strengths of Indonesian Families

In general, Indonesians have a well-deserved reputation for being warm, friendly, and genuine people. They are known to value patience and peaceful, nonconfrontational approaches to problem solving. They also tend to value conformity and group harmony. These attributes characterize relationships in general, but are certainly also present in parent-child relationships, which is a tremendous advantage in promoting children's well-being and success. Indonesians generally have strong family networks, which is also good for children. Grandparents often play an important role in caring for children, especially while parents work, treating grandchildren like their own children. Indonesians tend to value community wisdom, morals, and norms, and they take pains to teach their children about their cultural heritage, which builds children's sense of place and identity. This could include what's called *musyawara* (problem-solving discussions) and *gotong royong* (working together as a community, showing respect to elders, and being friendly to everyone). These are positive, prosocial interactions that build adaptive traits for children from any cultural background. And local distinctions in the ways families show their commitment to their children are even more important in considering program goals and design. For example, in North Sumatera, parents are known to be willing to literally sell the family farm to make sure their children go to school.

Although these strengths are generalizations that do not fit every family, they stem from truths. Clearly, families across Indonesia have a lot going for them; they bring many assets to the table, regardless of geography or economic situation. They are resources to appreciate and build on as program designers consider how to achieve their goals. It is extremely important for program designers and facilitators to recognize and encourage those traditions and values in parents—those strengths create the backbone for successful parenting programs.

Recent Research: A World Bank Impact Evaluation

Although we found no research that specifically aimed to evaluate parenting in Indonesia, the World Bank has completed a rigorously designed impact evaluation of an early childhood project in generally poor and rural districts across Indonesia. Focused on the impact of early childhood education programs, the project was not specifically designed to look at parenting per se, but it nonetheless sheds some light on the impact of parenting on children's well-being and success (Hasan, Hyson, and Chang 2013). The Indonesia Early Childhood Education and Development Project included over 500,000 children in 50 villages. The study designed to evaluate the project followed 6,000 of those children living in 310 villages in 9 districts of Indonesia between 2009 and 2013.

Empirical research often relies on two proxies—parents' education and wealth—to represent positive parenting practices. Although useful and relatively easy to measure, these proxies are not exact measures of what parents actually do, however. One can be wealthy and a negligent parent or can lack education but be a warm and loving parent, for example. The World Bank impact evaluation measured both the two proxies *and* parents' self-report of actual parenting practices and attitudes, using questions adapted from the Longitudinal Study of Australian Children (Zubrick et al. 2008). Mothers in the study were asked to answer 24 questions about their parenting practices and the parent-child relationship, measuring three critical aspects of parenting:

- *Warmth*—for example, "How often do you spend time with your child in a warm/friendly surrounding?"
- *Consistency*—for example, "When you discipline your child, how often does he/she ignore his/her punishment?"
- *Hostility*—for example, "How often are you angry with your child?"

Mothers were asked how often they used these and other parenting practices. The higher the overall score (with hostility scores reversed), the more likely it was that parents had high levels of warmth and consistency, and low levels of hostility toward their children—in other words, had better parenting practices. The researchers found that better parenting practices were associated with better nutrition practices (for example, providing milk and vegetables on a daily basis) and better knowledge (for example, knowing that a child should drink more fluids than normal during a bout of diarrhea, knowing where the location of the nearest early childhood development center).

Parenting practices were associated with child development, as well. Specifically, higher parenting scores correlated with lower child behavior problems and emotional problems, and with higher scores in all five domains of the Early Development Instrument (that is, physical health and well-being; social competence; emotional maturity; language and cognitive development; and communication skills and general knowledge). The results were statistically significant: The difference in children's language and cognitive development, for example, was one half standard deviation between the least good and the best parents. To put this in perspective consider that the difference in children's language and cognitive development between a stunted child (one who is severely malnourished) and one that is not is also one half standard deviation. Thus better parenting practices are as powerful in a positive direction as stunting is in a negative direction. It also compares with the strength of the relationship between children's participation in early childhood development services and positive outcomes.

Language and cognitive development are areas of particular concern for Indonesia, and although parenting practices were associated with child outcomes in these areas, the effects of early childhood development participation were stronger. However, parenting behaviors were more important than any other factor examined for impacting children's physical health. Moreover, these positive associations remained even after researchers controlled for parents' education and wealth; they found that positive parenting behaviors played a strong role in children's development above and beyond education and wealth. Furthermore, even after researchers controlled for children's enrollment in early childhood development services, parenting still played a unique and powerful role in children's well-being. In other words, parenting skills mattered.

Areas in Which Indonesian Parents Need Support

Although we were not able to find any large-scale empirical studies specifying Indonesian parents' needs, two reports based on anecdotal observations are useful in suggesting ways to support parents and improve parenting skills: (1) a Plan Indonesia situational analysis report from the Sikka and Lembata districts in Nusa Tenggara Timur (NTT) (Cahyono et al. 2010), and (2) a World Bank field visit report to Yogyakarta and North Sulawesi (Andina and Tomlinson 2013), related to the design of parenting education modules for the Ministry of Social Affairs' *Program Keluarga Harapan* /Family Development Sessions (PKH/FDS, discussed in Appendix A). From these two reports, we outline possible areas of need related to parenting education in Indonesia. First is the need to reduce the use of physical punishment, something not specifically named by parents as a problem but cited by observers as an area for improvement. And second are needs cited by the parents themselves, including children's health and safety, financial well-being, managing children's disobedience, and helping children achieve their ambitions.

Reducing Parents' Reliance on Physical Punishment

Before designing its parenting education program, Plan Indonesia conducted a situation analysis of its working areas in NTT. Observers noted a high incidence of corporal punishment among parents or threats of corporal punishment, suggesting that parents could use support in developing a "parenting style which didn't involve violence" (Cahyono et al. 2010, p. 44). Hitting was reported to be the primary means of disciplining children. These findings were echoed in the PKH field visit report from observations and focus group discussions in Yogyakarta and North Sulawesi, where pinching and ear twisting were cited as typical disciplinary tactics (Andina and Tomlinson 2013). Although parents do not necessarily ask for alternative ways to discipline children, child development specialists call for nonviolent approaches to managing children's behavior.

Protecting Children's Health and Safety

On the basis of focus group discussions, some mothers reported struggling with a child's refusal to eat nutritional foods or worry about a child who gets sick unusually often. One mother explained that her daughter developed epilepsy two years ago. So far, the seizures have occurred only while the child is sleeping, but she is quite concerned the child will have a seizure somewhere that it would be dangerous. Another mother was especially worried about her nine-year-old daughter who frequently walks to or from school. They family lives at the edge of a jungle, about 4 kilometers from school, too far for *ojek* (motorbike taxi) drivers to regularly come, so the daughter has to walk alone. Parents in Tikala said they worried about their children playing in or near the river during rainy season when the local river becomes quite high. They also noted that since the development of a major road in their village, several children have been hit by cars. They worry about their children both playing in the road and crossing the road without an adult. Keeping children healthy and safe from physical harm involves parents' knowledge and judgment.

Achieving Financial Well-Being

Another worry that keeps many mothers awake at night is family finances. Without exception, mothers (and children) interviewed during PKH site visits reported that mothers rather than fathers manage the family budget. Mothers reported worrying often about money—not only for immediate food, shelter, and clothing needs, but also for paying for education programs, whether at the early childhood or senior high school level. Mothers also reported worrying about what would happen if their husbands became sick or lost their jobs, which would reduce or wipe out their income. Almost all mothers in this population of poor parents reported having no savings. Some parenting education programs, such as the PKH/FDS program, help parents address household management or financial skills, which can improve material and emotional stability in a family.

Managing Disobedience and Difficult Requests

Repeatedly, parents said the hardest thing about being a parent is knowing what to do when a child misbehaves. When children refuse to take a bath, fight with a sibling, or will not get up on time to go to school, parents said they were unsure how to handle the situation. A mother explained that she has a neighbor watch the children when she goes to work at her hotel job; she worries the children will misbehave and the neighbor will get fed up and not watch the children anymore. When children misbehave, as previously mentioned, mothers reported pinching, twisting ears, and yelling. They reported separating fighting siblings or children. They also said they tell the child that the father, the teacher or Santa Claus (in Manado) will be angry with the child as a result of disobedience. Across groups, mothers reported no particular avenue for support or person from whom they received advice or help about these concerns. They said they try to solve family problems with their husband. They said very occasionally they might ask their own parent or a religious leader for parenting tips, but not teachers or health professionals. They also reported praying and "talking to the pillow" (that is, crying).

Reviewers from Plan Indonesia (2010) noted that the concept of "naughty behavior" for parents they observed and interviewed included being demanding; frequent crying or whining to get a desired object or money; disobedience, including wanting to play "all the time," playing far away from home, bringing friends home and making a mess; being aggressive, such as hitting or throwing items; having tantrums; and being irresponsible, including taking younger siblings to play away from the house and asking for money before school. Asking for money was noted as "the most common thing that children like to ask [for] from the parents" (p. 86). Reviewers quoted a parent as saying, "They [the children] don't want to take a bath until we give them money" (p. 86). Lack of knowledge, practical strategies, and trusted resource persons make topics in this category ripe for parenting education intervention.

Achieving Ambitions

Parents' ambitions for their children centered on them becoming good people and having higher levels of education (definitions of higher education ranged from some primary school to university). In terms of occupation, some mothers dreamed of their children becoming a professional—perhaps a teacher, priest, or doctor. Some mothers reported intentionally not sharing their dreams with their children for fear that children would rebel, lose motivation, and become "lazy." Some said they cared deeply about their children reaching their dreams and were worried about the children being disappointed if they failed. They said they try to support their children's success by helping them with homework and trying to motivate them to learn, making them do their homework, telling them to be diligent in school and to listen to their parents, and encouraging them to stay in school. Some mothers reported concerns about a child who was unusually quiet or different than other children, and not knowing how to "make them" more like the other children. Parents would benefit from information about specific and practical ways to support children's success in school, as well as general information about child development and knowing when to seek professional help about an intellectual or social problem.

Recommended Indonesia-Specific Content

The previous section described content that is frequently covered in parenting education programs. These components would be useful in Indonesia, but in addition, there are other content components that could be significant within the context of Indonesia, and for parents with low income and education levels in particular.

First, reports suggest that parents' sense of awareness of themselves as role models and self-efficacy as parents is low; that is, parents do not perceive themselves as being especially effective, powerful, or important. These parents need support to increase their confidence through encouragement, praise, and practical strategies and skills. Content that explicitly explains to parents how critical they are will do much to empower them, as well teaching them good general parenting practices and attitudes toward children. On the basis of the World Bank impact evaluation of the Early Childhood Education and Development project, teaching about or praising parents for warmth, consistency, and ability to control anger and hostility might be useful components of parenting programs, especially for parents with low self-esteem. Parents deserve to understand that they are the most powerful people in their children's lives, regardless of how much money or education they have or do not have.

Second, although there is a general philosophy that the early years are important—hence the name "the golden period"—there tends to be little awareness among low-socioeconomic families that parents should talk to, cuddle, and engage with children from birth onwards. Explicitly teaching parents about the value of play for young children could be a good strategy for enhancing parent–child bonds, reducing disciplinary problems, and increase cognitive and language skills. Backing up the rhetoric about play by teaching practical skills—learning new games, reviving traditional games, and creating toys and learning materials from local resources—would also benefit this population of parents. In addition, they deserve to recognize what a good early childhood education program does—it uses play to enhance children's social, language, and cognitive skills—so that children can be successful in school and later life.

In short, additional key messages relevant in Indonesia include (1) parents are vital role models for their children; (2) parents are powerful and important people in their children's lives, no matter how much money or education they have; (3) children need attention, conversation, affection, and stimulation from birth onwards to develop well; (4) children learn through play in the golden period of early childhood; and (5) early childhood education programs such as PAUD programs (preschools) are important for helping children develop social and cognitive skills to be successful in school.

In addition to building on families' strengths, as previously discussed, program designers should use solid, research-based approaches to creating effective parenting education programs, discussed in the next chapter.

CHAPTER 4

Existing Parenting Education Programs in Indonesia

Abstract

This chapter presents an overview of the parenting education programs we know about that are making an impact in Indonesia, either because of widespread coverage, innovative design, or potential for enhancing or scaling up. We then provide recommendations based on the big picture of parenting education as a system within and across the country. Recommendations for specific programs can be found in Appendix A: Parenting Education in Indonesia: Seven Program Examples from the Field, which provides detailed information about each program's goals and operations.

The Big Picture: Geographical Coverage

This section provides an overview of programs operating in Indonesia, four implemented by the government and three by nongovernmental organizations (NGOs): (1) the Ministry of Health's *Kelas Ibu* (Mother Class) program, (2) the National Board on Family Planning's *Bina Keluarga Balita* (BKB) program, (3) the Ministry of Social Affairs' two programs, *Taman Anak Sejahtera* (TAS) and *Program Keluarga Harapan/*Family Development Sessions (PKH/FDS), (4) the Ministry of Education and Culture's two new grant initiatives, (5) Plan Indonesia's parenting groups, *Kelompok Pengasuhan Anak* (KPA), (6) Save the Children's programs (variously called BLEND, BISA, SPECIAL, BELAJAR, and SETARA), and (7) World Vision's approach, *Wahana Pendidikan Anak Usia Emas* (Vehicle for the Golden Period of Early Education).

These programs collectively cover almost all areas of Indonesia, in theory—every province has or will have at least one parenting program, but those programs may only reach a handful of parents in one or a select few districts. As shown in map 4.1, some programs operate in all provinces, particularly the government-run programs such as *Badan Kependudukan dan Keluarga Berencana Nasional* (BKKBN)'s *Bina Keluarga Balita* (BKB) program, while others only

Map 4.1 Parenting Education Program Coverage in Indonesia

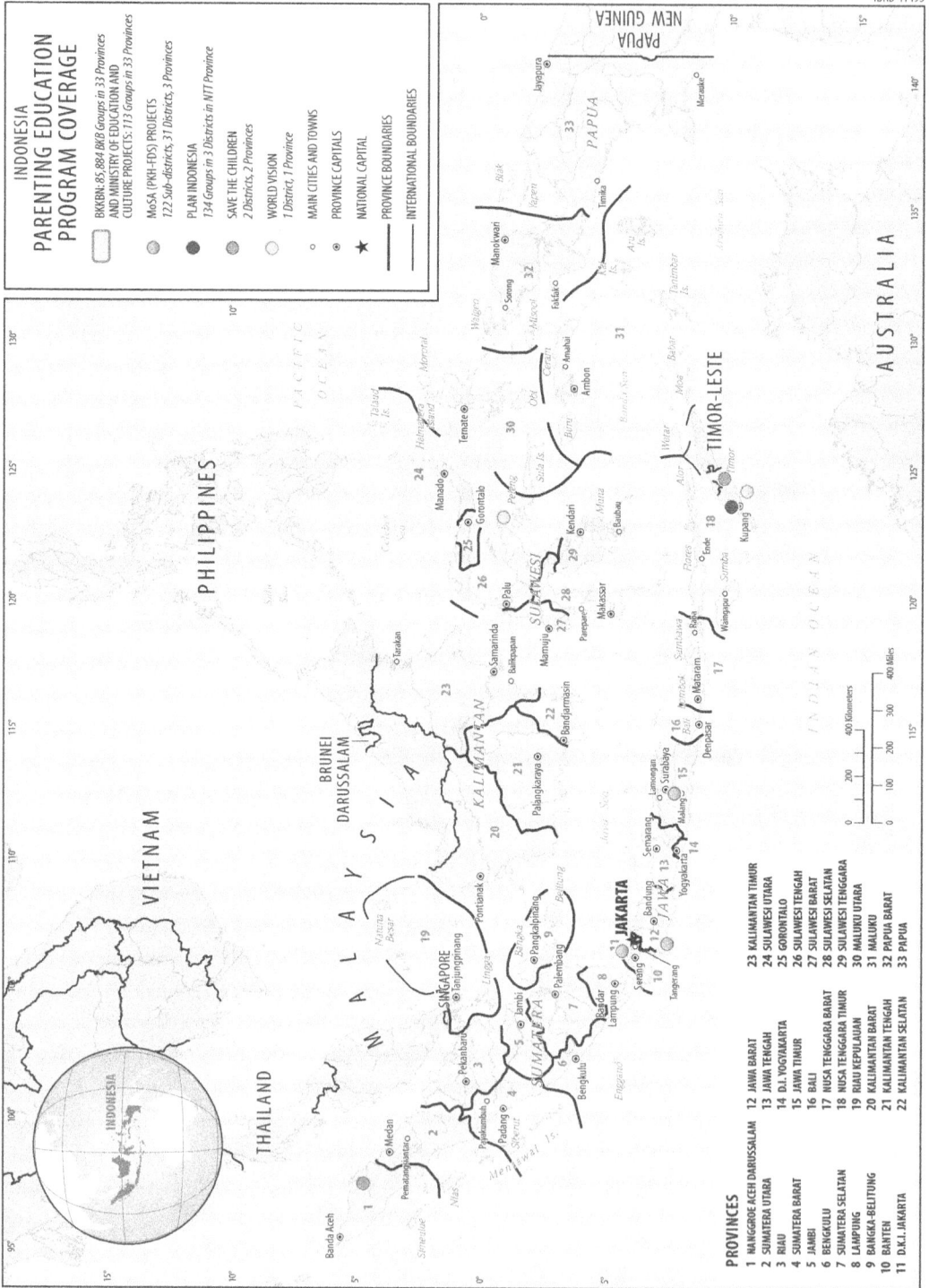

IBRD 41493

INDONESIA
PARENTING EDUCATION
PROGRAM COVERAGE

BKKBN: 85,884 BKB Groups in 33 Provinces
AND MINISTRY OF EDUCATION AND
CULTURE PROJECTS: 713 Groups in 33 Provinces

⬤ MoSA (PKH-FDS) PROJECTS
  122 Sub-districts, 31 Districts, 3 Provinces

⬤ PLAN INDONESIA
  134 Groups in 3 Districts in NTT Province

⬤ SAVE THE CHILDREN
  2 Districts, 2 Provinces

⬤ WORLD VISION
  1 District, 1 Province

○ MAIN CITIES AND TOWNS

⊙ PROVINCE CAPITALS

★ NATIONAL CAPITAL

── PROVINCE BOUNDARIES

── INTERNATIONAL BOUNDARIES

PROVINCES

1 NANGROE ACEH DARUSSALAM
2 SUMATERA UTARA
3 RIAU
4 SUMATERA BARAT
5 JAMBI
6 BENGKULU
7 SUMATERA SELATAN
8 LAMPUNG
9 BANGKA-BELITUNG
10 BANTEN
11 D.K.I. JAKARTA
12 JAWA BARAT
13 JAWA TENGAH
14 D.I. YOGYAKARTA
15 JAWA TIMUR
16 BALI
17 NUSA TENGGARA BARAT
18 NUSA TENGGARA TIMUR
19 RIAU KEPULAUAN
20 KALIMANTAN BARAT
21 KALIMANTAN TENGAH
22 KALIMANTAN SELATAN
23 KALIMANTAN TIMUR
24 SULAWESI UTARA
25 GORONTALO
26 SULAWESI TENGAH
27 SULAWESI BARAT
28 SULAWESI SELATAN
29 SULAWESI TENGGARA
30 MALUKU UTARA
31 MALUKU
32 PAPUA BARAT
33 PAPUA

MARCH 2015

Source: Data are based on information collected during interviews. Ministry of Health and Ministry of Social Affairs programs are not included because of lack of data.

Parenting Education in Indonesia • http://dx.doi.org/10.1596/978-1-4648-0621-6

operate in one or two provinces, such as World Vision's programs. And some programs, such as the new grants under Ministry of Education and Culture (MoEC), exist in all provinces, but only run one or two programs in each province, touching a mere handful of people. One important program absent from this map is the Ministry of Health (MoH) *Kelas Ibu* program, which is not included because the Ministry does not keep track at the national level of where the classes exist (funding and implementation occur at the district level). Ministry of Social Affairs (MoSA)'s two programs are also not included because its staff does not keep track of TAS parenting programs.

Regardless of whether coverage is vast or tiny, all the programs are important and have something to offer, both to families in their coverage areas and to our understanding of how to enact effective programs in Indonesia. What follows is a brief summary of the support mechanisms, goals, content, and structure of the programs considered, presented according to the supporting agency, with the programs of four government ministries discussed first, followed by three NGO programs. Fuller details on programs operations may be found in the appendices.

Government Programs

Four ministries provide parenting education programs of some type to parents in Indonesia. The two ministries with the biggest outreach historically were the Ministry of Health and BKKBN, although the Ministry of Social Affair's relatively new PKH/FDS program is emerging as an important program for reaching poor families. MoEC has historically not ventured into parenting education, but it is becoming active in the current administration with two new grant programs and a directorate focused specifically on parenting education. More specific information follows.

Ministry of Health

Indonesia's Ministry of Health plays a critical role in parenting education for women across Indonesia, particularly in relaying information about optimal breastfeeding, immunizations, hygiene, and safety practices for infants, toddlers, and young children. The national MoH office is the origin of two parenting education classes provided to mothers in all 33 provinces across the county: *Kelas Ibu Hamil* (classes for pregnant women) and *Kelas Ibu Balita* (classes for mothers of children younger than five years old), collectively referred to as *Kelas Ibu* or Mother Classes. District health offices must offer these classes to community residents, with initial contact with women occurring primarily through *posyandu* (village health post providing integrated services) and *puskesmas* (health center usually serving several villages). Staff focuses on mother and child health issues, especially as they relate to physical health: labor and delivery, breastfeeding, immunizations, safe and hygienic environments, and preventing and treating illnesses. Facilitators also may provide some information about children's developmental milestones in areas other than physical health, such as social-emotional and cognitive areas, although these aspects are secondary to the physical health messages.

Facilitators are usually *kaders*, who are paraprofessional health workers within villages. They receive some training from province health office staff but are not paid. They sometimes invite specialized professionals to speak to their parenting groups or serve as resource persons and receive some supervision and support from midwives or other health office personnel. Classes are held once per month for 1–1.5 hours and typically include about 10–15 mothers—although this number may be higher, depending on the area. Programs sometimes occur through *puskesmas* as well as *posyandu* and there is no standardized number of classes per cohort. Children may or may not be present during the meetings, depending on mothers' child care options. There are no data on who attends and for how long, although anecdotal evidence suggests mothers of younger children are more likely to attend than mothers of older children. Facilitators decide what topics to focus on during the classes, using the maternal and child health Handbook (MCH), often called "the pink book," as their guide. The pink book consists of about 60 pages of clear, simple messages conveyed by text and illustrations; it also has record charts in the back for a child's history of illnesses, development problems, growth status, and immunizations. The national office prints about 4.5 million pink books per year, enough to provide for 80 percent of the women expected to become pregnant in a given year. MoH has a wide reach because of its contact through health clinics with almost all poor and middle-income women in every district in the country. However, there are no data on the actual provision of and participation in *kelas ibu* or effectiveness of the classes.

National Board on Family Planning (BKKBN)

Badan Kependudukan dan Keluarga Berencana Nasional (BKKBN), the National Board on Family Planning, is viewed as a leader in terms of parenting education for young children in Indonesia, partly by reputation and partly by regulation. Government guidelines convey BKKBN authority for both implementing holistic, integrated early childhood development (ECD) programs (*Pedoman Umum PAUDHI*) and for overseeing parenting education programs, among their other responsibilities (BKKBN also provides services for families of adolescents and families caring for elderly family members). BKKBN offers parenting classes called *Bina Keluarga Balita* (BKB, Building Families of Young Children Groups). BKB programs reach parents in most districts and provide comprehensive content and messages that reflect all domains of child development in age-specific ways for children from ages zero to six years. It is not clear, even with the BKKBN organization, whether BKB programs target poor and rural families in particular or are available to a broader audience of parents. The program organizers often try to coordinate with ancillary service providers, such as *posyandus*.

BKB facilitators also often coordinate with local playgroups or other ECD programs, and parents meet while children experience their own ECD program.

Women become facilitators or *kaders* by invitation from leaders within the community (the selection criteria are unclear), and they may or may not hold other jobs as well. They receive training to use the BKKBN-provided guidebook, reading materials, and child development chart, and sometimes the training is integrated with training for PAUD staff, posyandu, and other program personnel. Government officials provide some supervision to the facilitators, who sometimes receive transportation reimbursement but are not paid. (Government officials receive a monthly salary, which not contingent upon these supervisory activities.)

Although facilitators were initially meant to provide nine classes to each group of participating parents, this number is not standardized in practice. Sessions might occur once per week, every fortnight, or once per month. BKB classes are designed for parents, not for children per se, although children sometimes attend the sessions with their parents, especially the younger children and especially when BKB classes for parents are held in the same room at the same time as the ECD program for children.

BKKBN is one of the few agencies for whom data are available, and the Board has recently commissioned both surveys and external evaluations of their BKB program. There are 84,000 BKB programs across the country, with 3.7 million member families with children younger than five years old. Therefore, on average, each BKB group has an average of 44 members. Researchers conducted a national survey using block sampling in 2012 to examine households served by BKKBN. Results showed that of 42,000 households sampled, 13,500 households consisted of families with children younger than five years old. Of those, 16 percent (about 2,100) attended BKB programs within the previous three months. This suggests that although there are 3.7 million families with young children that are members of BKB, only a fraction may actively participate in BKB programs. Although participation rates were lower than BKKBN and others expected, the survey revealed positive effects from the parenting classes: Parents reported they more actively supported children's creativity and play, intentionally acted as role models, worked to increase children's gratitude and respectfulness, and better protected children's physical health as a result of the program (see Appendix A for more details).

External evaluations of materials and program implementation were less flattering, however. In support of the program, they noted observations of parents' gains in knowledge about child development and reduced use of physical punishment. Evaluators cited several problems with materials, however, including the need to simplify the language, use more illustrations, be more consistent with the goals for young children, and to provide a more useful means of charting child growth and development. In particular, they found the Child Development Chart (KKA) to be confusing and not well used by facilitators or parents. Evaluators found the capacity of facilitators to be relatively low and parents' application of new knowledge at home limited. Another concern is the high turnover rate among *kaders* (reported to be 70 percent during conference proceedings).

Although the evaluators recommended revising the materials, BKKBN leadership has chosen not to revise the materials at this time. Instead, two sets of new materials have been developed. The first is a book for background reading for *kaders* called *Orangtua Pintar* or "Being a Smart Parent." The second is a set of eight books developed by the United Nations Children's Fund (UNICEF) and BKKBN, which BKKBN homes to distribute to 5.6 million families in 2014. Development of the two sets of materials was not coordinated but rather emerged simultaneously through different mechanisms within the agency, therefore the content is not intentionally aligned but has some overlap. Although the "Smart Parent" book was developed for facilitators in mind and the set of booklets was developed for distribution to parents, both sets of materials will likely be used by both facilitators and parents. BKKBN plans to create a credentialing process for facilitators using the new materials. It is not yet clear whether BKB programs will continue to receive the original materials as well as the new materials, or how distribution and training will take place.

In addition to the new materials, Bappenas is giving Rp 94 million in grant money in 2014 to BKKBN to support and strengthen selected BKB programs in 12 provinces.

Ministry of Education and Culture

The Ministry of Education and Culture (MoEC) has responsibility for managing the basic education system from primary school through junior secondary and secondary school. However, MoEC also plays an increasingly important role in the early childhood education system, including in the intersection with parenting education, through its ECD directorate-general. MoEC oversees kindergarten, playgroups, day care (TPA), and other early childhood programs such as Satuan PAUD Sejenis (SPS); provides guidelines for facilities, monitoring and evaluation, and training; and provides some financial support for the ECD system by helping with centers' operational costs. However, MoEC has not historically been involved in parenting education per se, which was seen more as the purview of other ministries, BKKBN and MoSA in particular. In 2013, the ministry was actively participating in parenting education through two grant initiatives. In January 2015, the ministry established a parenting education directorate, a valuable step in strengthening services.

Grant Programs

MoEC's structure for providing the grants is through existing PAUD (ECD) programs that submit successful proposals to create a parenting education program for parents at their ECD center. MoEC officials designed the first grant program, initially implemented in 2013, to reach parents of children from birth to age six years. They intend for the second grant program, in the final stages of development but not yet implemented, to target parents of children from birth to age three years. Although officials expect to see the first grant initiative expand to reach all 33 provinces in 2014, it will support only one program in each province (33 programs in total). In contrast, the zero to three grant initiative will also reach all 33 provinces but will support 80 programs in total.[1]

Each program receives Rp 25 million (US$2,500) directly from the ministry to spend within the year. The parenting classes are free for participating parents. Program staff may use the money to provide the parenting classes (for example, transportation for resource persons, meals, renting chairs), encourage parenting participation in the ECD program (for example, providing snacks for parents' days), purchase parent learning materials, buy supplies such as stationary and microphones, and receive coaching from the district office. Facilitators may be ECD teachers, health personnel, or religious leaders. Guidelines for facilitators are still being drafted, as well as goals for parenting behaviors. At present, there is no training or set of guidelines for facilitators.

One noteworthy component of the initiative for parents of infants and toddlers is that it will require parents to interact with their children (*pengasuhan bersama*) during the parenting class. This is unique among all the programs we have reviewed, as the only program to intentionally schedule in-session interaction between parents and children. Programs must spend 25 percent of their grant money on indoor toys and materials with which parents and children can play together during sessions and 10 percent on outdoor play equipment.

New Directorate General of Parenting Education

MoEC has established a new directorate general for parenting education as of January 2015. The directorate will provide online support via an interactive website to assist parents who want to better understand school curricula and support their children's success in school. It is not yet known what the specific aims of the directorate will be and whether other services will also be offered, but early indications suggest the purview of the directorate will focus on gains in education specifically, per the expertise of the ministry.

MoEC has a unique capacity to reach all families through its vast network of education personnel and knowledge of idiosyncratic needs and contexts of every district in the country. In contrast to various other programs that target poor families, MoEC has the capacity to reach families of all backgrounds by working through ECD programs. The new directorate for parenting education will sit under the Directorate General of Early Education, providing an opportunity to impact school readiness and transition to school success, among other goals.

Ministry of Social Affairs

Kementrian Sosial (*Kemensos*) is the Ministry of Social Affairs (MoSA) and, along with BKKBN, is entrusted by the greater government to have authority over parenting education. It provides two parenting education programs, each under a different directorate. The first, under the Directorate of Child Social Welfare (and the Sub-Directorate of Child Protection), is *Taman Anak Sejahtera* (TAS); the second, under the Directorate of Social Assurance (*Direktorat Jaminan Sosial*), is the *Program Keluarga Harapan*/Family Development Sessions (PKH/FDS). The former has been involved in parenting education longer but never developed modules; the latter has only recently become involved in parenting education but has defined modules. The two directorates have not yet collaborated but may do so in the future, and the TAS program will adopt the PKH/FDS modules for use in its program.

Taman Anak Sejahtera

Taman Anak Sejahtera (*TAS*) could be translated as Gardens for Children's Welfare. This program operates under *Program Kesejahteraan Sosial Anak* (PKSA), which is the ministry's social welfare program for children from 0–5. TAS programs consist of an existing ECD center—a PAUD, orphanage, day care program, or urban care center—that provides a parenting education component. MoSA gives Rp 1.5 million per year to the center to implement its parenting education component, plus Rp 100,000 per child for operational expenses. Not all children at the center receive funds; rather, district social workers decide which at-risk children should receive the funds. At-risk children could include children in poor families, street children, orphans, children in single-parent families, abused children, children with disabilities, victims of disasters, and so forth. Therefore, 5 out of 25 children may be TAS beneficiaries, for example.

There are 650 facilitators and they have served 8,000 children in 22 provinces. Facilitators are PKSA staff, who works together with the selected children's parents to decide how to spend the funds to best support the child. One of the ways staff may decide to spend the money is on the parenting education sessions. The sessions are generally open to all parents at the program, not only the selected children. There are not prescribed guidelines or requirements about how often to meet or what to discuss. Although Child Protection officials at MoSA had planned to develop modules, they have now decided to adapt the the four PKH/FDS parenting-skills modules (in addition to developing some new content for special populations, such as parents of special needs children), which are discussed next. Training for PKSA facilitators to use the developed modules is underway.

Program Keluarga Harapan Family Development Sessions (PKH/FDS)

The *Program Keluarga Harapan* (PKH or Family Hope Program), Indonesia's flagship poverty reduction program, consists of a conditional cash transfer system in which parents in poor households receive payments for participating in certain health and education activities. The overarching goal is to provide immediate financial relief to poor families while encouraging behavior changes and long-term health and productivity to disrupt intergenerational cycles of poverty. The program currently reaches 3 million poor families across the country.

Until recently, the program did not pay attention to the education and stimulation of young children before they reach primary school. To redress that missing piece, MoSA commissioned UNICEF and the World Bank to develop parenting education classes (Family Development Sessions) for PKH recipients. The sessions focus on a range of topics to be delivered to parents, including (1) health and nutrition, (2) child protection, (3) financial literacy, and (4) parenting skills to support children's social-emotional and cognitive development. UNICEF developed the content for sessions related to health, nutrition, and child protection, and the World Bank developed the content for financial literacy and parenting skills related to young children's care, stimulation, and education. (The authors of the current study developed the parenting skills modules.)

Participants—existing PKH beneficiaries who were eligible for PKH based on poverty status—attend 14 2- or 2.5-hour sessions over 14 months, meetings being held once per month. (This includes four sessions on parenting education per se, followed by sessions on economic well-being, health and nutrition, and child protection, which comprise the remaining 10 sessions. PKH/FDS facilitators are existing PKH facilitators who previously focused mainly on administrative components of managing PKH through regular meetings of 30–100 or more parents. In the new format, meetings now include administrative information (for example, about payment dates and requirements) *and* new content information (for example, about positive discipline techniques or the importance of playing with children). As of the beginning of 2015, 433 facilitators had received training to implement the modules. Meetings in the new format encourage a group size of 25–30 parents. Historically, mothers comprised the majority of participants. At present, facilitators should invite both mothers and fathers to encourage father participation. It is expected that some children will attend some classes with their parents, as they traditionally have, but their presence is not required.

There are clear guidelines and prescribed activities for facilitators to follow in sequence within each of the following four modules:

1. *Good Parenting*—having a positive self-image and the importance of fathers and parenting as a team;
2. *Understanding Children's Behavior*—how to increase children's good behavior and decrease bad behavior (without using physical punishment);
3. *Playing and Learning Go Together*—the importance of playing and learning at home and how to support children's language and literacy at home; and
4. *Success in School*—the importance of preschool and how to help children succeed in school.

Facilitators are trained to employ active learning techniques, such that parents frequently have small-group discussions, time for reflection, games to play to reinforce key messages, and homework to do between sessions.

Implementation of the modules began in November 2014. By early 2015, implementation had started in 122 *kecamatan* (subdistricts). MoSA coordinated with the National Development Planning Agency (Bappenas) and the World Bank to design monitoring and evaluation plans, using a randomized control trial approach. To provide comparison data, 122 *kecamatan* are participating as control groups.

Nongovernmental Organizations

Three nongovernmental organizations (NGOs) are active in providing parenting education programs or materials for parenting education programs in Indonesia. Whereas they do not have the financial strength or oversight roles of any ministerial body, they nonetheless provide essential services in parenting education, and have potential to reach even more people within the framework of a strengthened and cohesive system.

Plan International in Indonesia

Plan, an international humanitarian, child-centered organization, is in the midst of implementing its Community Managed Early Childhood Care and Development (CMECCD) program for the five-year period from 2012 to 2017, with a special emphasis on improving services for the 2.5 million school-aged children with disabilities. The organization believes that ownership and sustainability result from working through existing institutions, so it mobilizes local communities in managing services. It also maintains links with ministerial and international partners.

Plan operates its ECCD program in the Nusa Tenggara Timur (NTT) Province in Eastern Indonesia. The organization works in underdeveloped and isolated areas of the province and the target population are the poor within those areas. Within the project, one of four components is a parenting education program called *Kelompak Pengasuhan Anak* (KPA).[2] KPA is the entry point for the greater ECCD project, and is aimed at empowering parents, giving them higher levels of knowledge about and skills with child rearing. The intent of the ECCD program is to address all important domains of child development, including social-emotional, motor, cognitive, and language domains. At present, there are 134 KPA groups in three districts: Sikka (82), Lembata (44), and Kefa (8).

Paid Plan staff train volunteer posyandu kaders or parents, who then serve as facilitators. Facilitators, who do receive a structured set of step-by-step guidelines from which to work, are chosen according to their abilities, level of commitment, attitudes of inclusive towards all family members. Plan supports facilitators to engage in the following activities with or for parents: (1) building awareness; (2) growing commitment; (3) improving knowledge and skills; (4) applying learning and practices at home; and (5) monitoring, supporting, coaching, and spreading improved behavior.

An important philosophical distinction between the Plan approach and other parenting education approaches is that parents are not meant to view facilitators as "the experts" (in most other programs, especially government-run programs, facilitators are expected to have some knowledge and skills to impart to parent participants). Instead, the goal is for parents to teach each other. There are facilitator guidelines—developed for use in multiple countries but adapted to Indonesia—which provide topics for discussion and background reading materials, but facilitators are encouraged to use the materials loosely, remain flexible, and explore how parents can identify their own goals and effective parenting strategies.

Groups, consisting of 15–30 parents, meet once per month for 10 months for about 2 hours. *Posyandu* are the most typical venue for the group meetings. Parents may have children ranging in age from birth to eight years. Most participants are mothers, but fathers are encouraged to come and sometimes separate groups for fathers emerge (13 in the last year). Facilitators are responsible for running at least five parenting groups per year. Facilitators may also offer longer-running and or/more intensive groups. Beyond the groups, facilitators also conduct home visits.

At the completion of the sessions, facilitators invite parents to continue to meet to determine whether they wish to take collective action to improve children's well-being in the community. On average, groups take one to three sessions to come up with a plan they wish to implement in the community, using its own budget for implementing any plans. Eighty-seven percent of groups implemented an action plan.

Plan commissioned a rigorous pilot study of its KPA programs in Sikka and Lembata (Agarwal-Harding et al. 2014). Findings suggested that parents indeed improved in knowledge, attitudes, and time spent with their children. Intervention groups showed higher levels than control groups of child stimulation and child protection, and decreased levels of harsch discipline. On the basis of self-report, 576 out of 613 parents reported using at least one new practice at home (for example, playing with children, washing hands, using positive discipline). Group differences in levels of nutrition and health knowledge remained unchanged by the program. External reviewers noted several strengths of KPA groups, such as its practical and user-friendly approach and affordability, among other things. In terms of recommendations, reviewers suggested strengthening health content; inviting children to participate in sessions; increasing the frequency of contact between facilitators and parents; improve faciltitators' ability to collect data; and engaging the government to formalize partnerships and expand the program.

Save the Children in Indonesia

Save the Children is an international nongovernmental organization that promotes children's rights and tries to improve children's lives by improving services in education, health care, child protection, and emergency aid sectors in 120 countries. In Indonesia, it has programs in 14 provinces using support from private donors and international development agencies. Staff sees parenting meetings as a critical avenue for enhancing children's well-being, especially in poor and rural areas. Rural areas of Aceh (two programs) and and NTT (three programs) serve as the focus points for their interventions related to parent engagement (see Appendix A for more details).

Parent meetings most often take place at ECD centers and usually occur once per month for one to two hours. Save the Children supports five sessions over five months, after which its involvement ends, but it encourages the community to continue to run the programs independently. ECD teachers play an important role in organizing the meetings and inviting parents, but Save the Children facilitators (called Master Trainers) run the sessions initially. Facilitators do not have guidelines or curricula to follow; they meet monthly with each other to decide what to discuss in their respective groups, sometimes with input from national office staff. They discuss the preselected topic using a combination of lecture, games, discussions, and question-and-answer approaches. They also conduct home visits.

Participants, parents of children attending the ECD program, include mothers and fathers but not children. There are usually 30–25 people per group. Facilitators, unlike in many other programs in Indonesia, are not community health workers or local consultants, but rather they are ECD teachers, program directors, or school supervisors. (Staff found that teachers made better facilitators than those in supervisory roles and so the number of directors and supervisors has diminished.) They receive a five-day training on basic information about young children, followed a year later by a three-day training (in Aceh only) on parenting education. In addition to running the parenting meetings and working their "day jobs," facilitators also provide technical assistance to teachers. They receive transportation reimbursements but no salary.

Facilitators have monthly evaluation meetings based on their observations, although they do not use standardized data forms to collect information. They report that parent attendance is high, and national Plan staff has observed positive effects from the parent meetings, such as increased ECD participation, more parent involvement with ECD programs, and more homemade toys and ideas for interacting with children. Staff hope to increase attention to infants and toddlers in the future, though primarily to focus on feeding practices.

World Vision International in Indonesia

World Vision is a faith-based, nongovernmental, nonprofit organization that promotes a Christian philosophy while working to improve the lives of children of any background. It has offices in more than 100 countries. In Indonesia, its priorities for young children have traditionally focused soley on children's physical health, but has a newly holistic approach to children's well-being that also includes attention to children's stimulation and education needs. The holistic philosophy is only reflected in current program goals for young children as of 2014; before this year, objectives broadly focused on ensuring children were well-nourished and protected against disease and infection.

World Vision's local offices, called area development programs, are located in 51 poor communities in 6 regions. They serve at least 85,000 children and families—although only a handful of those recieve parenting sessions. Area development program staff members work with community members to decide how best to support their respective communities, partnering with local groups and consultants. Because each community comes up with its own goals and activities, there is no standardized parenting education program—but at least 8 out of the

51 area development programs report having projects related to ECD, some of which include parenting education programs (for example, Surabaya, Poso, Alor). This is the *Wahana Pendidikan Anak Usia Emas* (Vehicle for the Golden Period of Early Education) approach.

Using World Vision International modules, the area development programs adapt the messages to local context. There are 72 modules from which to choose, covering a variety of topics on children's comprehensive needs: Calming your baby, showing love and affection, immunizations and supplements, learning through play, developing self-esteem, deworming, treating each other with care and respect, learning to communicate better, starting school, being careful of strangers, learning to read and write, and preventing domestic violence are a few examples of the topics facilitators may choose to discuss. Module guidelines, which are downloaded from a centralized website, are about four pages long, written in basic language, include photos, provide clear message content, and give ideas for in-session activities.

There is no standard approach to organizing parenting sessions, the sequence of topics, group size, type of participants included, or length of meetings. Facilitators are area development program staff members and/or *posyandu kaders*, with a heavy reliance on local consultants from schools, universities, or NGOs. Staff typically use a bidding process through which they choose consultants, who must use the World Vision modules as the basis for their discussions with parents. Area development program staff members receive a salary, but consultants may or may not receive any payment, an issue determined locally.

Given the idiosyncratic nature of program implementation, there are no data to evaluate effectiveness of the parenting programs. National staff indicate coming priorities will include a focus on the frequency and quality of parent-child interactions.

Programs at a Glance: Two Matrices

The two matrices (tables 4.1 and 4.2) offer another way to consider and compare the programs. Table 4.1 outlines aspects of program content and table 4.2 outlines aspects of program design and delivery. In terms of content, covering more topics is not necessarily better, as it may create programs that are "a mile wide and an inch deep," meaning that they are too broad to impact any one particular area of parenting. Although the number of topics covered does not convey quality of implementation, it does show the range of materials already available for general populations and adapted to the Indonesian language and culture.

Table 4.1 Content Components of Parenting Education Programs

Content	Program name							
	MoH	MOEC	MOSA		BKKBN	Plan International	Save the Children	World Vision
	Kelas Ibu	37 booklets	TAS	PKH/FDS	BKB	KPA		
	The MCH handbook ("pink book") focuses primarily on health and feeding practices, with additional information on developmental milestones for children from birth to age 5 years.	Booklets are comprehensive but not well used and cover a broader range of topics than necessary for MoEC. The two grant programs may or may not involve booklets, not specified.	There are no materials at present; officials will adapt four PKH/FDS parenting modules; they may develop more modules.	There are 12 modules, 4 of which relate to parenting per se, described here (others are health and nutrition, child protection, budgeting).	Evaluators have determined materials are not well understood by facilitators or parents, particularly child development (KKA) checklist.	Facilitators' manual provides background reading materials on these topics, adapted for use in various countries.	Materials are background reading for facilitators.	There are 72 modules available online; can be adapted internationally; they are well designed, attractive and practical, but there is no systematic or widespread use in Indonesia.
Knowledge of Child Development and Care[a]	✓	✓			✓	✓	✓	✓
Positive Interaction with Children		✓		✓	✓			✓
Emotional Communication		✓		✓	✓	✓	✓	✓

table continues next page

Parenting Education in Indonesia • http://dx.doi.org/10.1596/978-1-4648-0621-6

Table 4.1 Content Components of Parenting Education Programs (continued)

			Program name				
	MoH	MOEC	MOSA		BKKBN	Plan International	Save the
Content	Kelas Ibu	37 booklets	TAS	PKH/FDS	BKB	KPA	Children	World Vision
Discipline and Behavior Management		✓		✓	✓	✓		✓
Promoting Children's Social Skills and Pro-Social Behavior		✓		✓	✓	✓		✓
Promoting Children's Cognitive and Academic Skills		✓		✓	✓	✓		✓
Self-Awareness as Parents: Being Warm, Consistent, and Not Hostile				✓	✓			✓
Promoting Play and Toy Making		✓		✓		✓	✓	

Note: BKB = *Bina Keluarga Balita*; BKKBN = *Badan Kependudukan dan Keluarga Berencana Nasional*; KKA = *Kartu Kemajuan Anak* (Child Development Chart); KPA = *Kelompok Pengasuhan Anak*; MOEC = Ministry of Education and Culture; MoH = Ministry of Health; MOSA = Ministry of Social Affairs; PKH/FDS = *Program Keluarga Harapan Family Development Sessions*; TAS = *Taman Anak Sejahtera*.
a. Includes a wide range of topics, such as knowledge of developmental milestones, good feeding practices, creating safe environments for children, and more, though only some topics may be represented in a given program.

Table 4.2 Design and Delivery Components of Parenting Education Programs

Design and delivery	MoH — *Kelas Ibu*	MOEC — *Grants and 37 booklets*	*TAS*	MOSA — *PKH/FDS*	BKKBN — *BKB*	Plan International — *KPA*	*Save the Children*	*World Vision*
Targeted population of parents	Pregnant mothers, mothers of children younger than 5 years using *posyandu* services	Parents of children enrolled in an ECD program	Parents of at-risk children who participate in TAS ECD programs	Poor parents enrolled in the PKH poverty-reduction program	Parents of children from birth to 6 years	Parents of children from birth to 8 years in poor communities	Parents of children younger than 6 years old in poor communities	Parents in poor communities
Targeted child age	Prenatal stage up to children 5 years old	Grant funds for children from birth to 6 years and from birth to 3 years	Birth to 8 years	Parents may have children up to age 14 years	Birth to 6 years	Birth to 8 years	Birth to 6 years	Birth to 6 years
Typical group size and participants	10–15 mothers	Not standardized	Not standardized	Designed for 25–30 parents	Not standardized	Maximum 30 parents	Not standardized	Not standardized
Frequency and duration of sessions	Once a month, 1–1.5 hours	Once a month, maximum 2 hours	Not standardized	Once per month, 2 hours	Once per month, maximum 2 hours	Once per month, 1.5–2 hours	Once per month, maximum 2 hours	Not standardized
Program goals are explicitly stated	No	No	No	Yes	No	No	No	No
Active learning for adults (participatory)	Not standardized	Not yet determined	Not standardized	Group discussion, role playing, games, testimony, homework	Group discussion, role playing	Group Discussion, role play, games	Not standardized	Not standardized, but discussion and activities are suggested
In-session practice between parents and children	Not required	Required for 0–3 years old (new grant)	Not standardized	Not required	Sometimes occurs but not required	Not required	Not standardized	Not standardized

table continues next page

Parenting Education in Indonesia • http://dx.doi.org/10.1596/978-1-4648-0621-6

Table 4.2 Design and Delivery Components of Parenting Education Programs *(continued)*

Design and delivery	MoH — Kelas Ibu	MOEC — Grants and 37 booklets	MOSA — TAS	MOSA — PKH/FDS	BKKBN — BKB	Plan International — KPA	Save the Children	World Vision
Availability of facilitator guidelines	Yes (content and activities)	No	No	Yes (content and activities)	Yes (content only)	Yes (content and suggested activities)	No	Yes (content and suggested activities)
In-session materials	Flipchart	Slide presentation	Not applicable	Flipchart, videos, brochure, poster	Flipchart, discussion cards, toys	Not applicable	Slide presentation	Not applicable
Facilitators	Health personnel at *puskesmas* or *posyandu*	Teachers, various resources person	PKSA staff (social workers)	PKH facilitators	BKB *kaders* (community volunteer)	Plan staff and volunteer kaders	Education officer; teachers	World Vision Staff;teachers
Facilitator incentives/salary	Transportation allowance only	Not usually, though may occur	Nothing extra, paid only as PKSA facilitator	Nothing extra, paid as PKH facilitators	Transportation allowance sometimes	No	Transportation allowance only	Only area development program staff members receive salaries
Facilitator training	5 days of pre service training conducted by provincial trainer using MoH training guidelines	Not yet standardized	Not yet standardized	Training of trainers by World Bank (5 days), MOSA Master Trainers will train facilitators starting April 2014	Conducted by trainers at the province level	5 days of pre-service training conducted by country office Plan staff	Conducted by Save the Children staff at the national level	Conducted by World Vision staff at the national level, but not specific to parenting groups
Monitoring and evaluation	Record number of MCH books, flipcharts printed; no data on number of programs; evaluate facilitators during training	Not yet standardized	Not yet standardized	Baseline data and impact evaluations will occur by either World Bank or TNP2K; will include parent outcomes	PLKB (BKKBN officials) collect data on attendance at parent meetings	Selected families receive home visits at which Plan staff observe and collect self-report information on parenting behaviors	No national data on program effectiveness	No national data on number of programs or program effectiveness (local programs may develop their own evaluations, unknown)

Note: BKB = *Bina Keluarga Balita;* BKKBN = *Badan Kependudukan dan Keluarga Berencana Nasional;* ECD = Early Childhood Development; KKA = *Kartu Kemajuan Anak* (Child Development Chart); KPA = *Kelompok Pengasuhan Anak;* MOEC = Ministry of Education and Culture; MoH = Ministry of Health; MOSA = Ministry of Social Affairs; PKH/FDS = *Program Keluarga Harapan Family Development Sessions;* PKSA = *Program Kesejahteraan Sosial Anak;* PLKB = *Petuagas Lapangan Keluarga Berencana* (BKKBN officials); TAS = *Taman Anak Sejahtera;* TNP2K = *Tim Nasional Percepatan Penanggulangan Kemiskinan* (Indonesia National Team for the Acceleration of Poverty Reduction).

In Closing

The programs described operate in varied and informative ways. They are varied in their approaches to program creation and operations (some are highly structured, others loosely emerge from parent input); funding (sources include ministries, private donors, international NGOs); target populations (mothers of newborns, parents of children in ECD programs, poor families); approach to pedagogy (some rely primarily on lectures, others are interactive); and facilitator selection and support (some facilitators go through formal interview or bidding processes, others are ECD teachers, others are *posyandu* staff). These differences reveal creativity, practicality, and deference to local resources and needs.

The programs also are informative because of their commonalities. There are many aspects of the programs that appear in most or all of the programs, painting a picture of what is collectively Indonesian in terms of parenting education programs. Most programs serve families with children across a wide age span, from babies in the womb to children up to six or eight years old; they cover a wide array of topics; they show cohesion based on group discussion; they occur for about two hours once per month; they are generally led by facilitators who recieve some training but no pay; they value oral communication over written communication, including for data collection and program improvment. These commonalities tell us something about the values of people designing the programs as well as limitations constraining them in terms of knowledge, financial resources, or both. On the basis of these variations and commonalities, the next section presents some overarching considerations and recommendations.

Notes

1. At the time of publication of this report in June 2015, plans to implement the MoEC grant program for infants and toddlers had been canceled.
2. The four components include improving parenting practices; strengthening ECCD Centers and Posyandu facilitators; increasing transition to primary school; and promoting advocacy/partnerships.

CHAPTER 5

Discussion and Recommendations

Introduction

There is a dynamic and growing energy in Indonesia around parenting education programs, as government officials, donor agencies, international nongovernmental organizations (NGOs), and community leaders recognize the power of parenting education programs to transform lives and therefore communities. The number of programs discussed and the variety of people involved in implementation of programs in Indonesia underscores the interest in this as an avenue to affect change at a particularly important time in family life, when children are young and experiences and interactions matter a great deal.

Early childhood is a challenging period around which to create policy because of its inherently multisectoral nature—although saying as much does a disservice to the naturally integrated way children grow, learn, and experience well-being. From the prenatal period onwards, physical health and growth is an obvious issue for policymakers to tackle, especially in a country such as Indonesia where maternal and infant mortality, stunting, weight gain, lack of consistently safe water supply, poor hygiene habits, and preventable childhood illnesses are still challenging issues. Yet, the psychosocial and cognitive domains of development are equally critical and frequently overlooked in the early years in many countries, including Indonesia, where young children's stimulation is not always considered important—an issue reflected in relatively poor cognitive scores and later school achievement. The intersections of health, social-emotional, and cognitive well-being for young children exist centrally within the interactions and attachments between children and their parents. As such, and given the research on effective parenting education programs, we make the following observations and recommendations regarding Indonesia's programs as a whole.

On a positive note, the content of program materials across the various programs is shifting toward this holistic view of children's development, which is encouraging. All of the programs considered included content on children's holistic needs in health, social-emotional, and cognitive domains. Because of Indonesia's historically poor performance relative to some Millennium

Development Goals in health areas—particularly maternal and child mortality and hunger manifest in the incidence of stunting—many of the programs are stronger in the health content as compared to the social-emotional and cognitive content. The most obvious example is the Ministry of Health (MoH) *Kelas Ibu* program which historically only focused on pregnant women's health and babies' growth related to breastfeeding, although it now includes developmental milestones and tips for stimulating children's development. Most programs do now include messages about various areas of child development.

There are many commonalities across the various programs discussed, perhaps saying more about the circumstances, current values, or available resources than any particular program. Our recommendations to improve current programs in general, regardless of the provider, follow.

Strengthening Program Content

This study has described seven approaches to parenting education. Almost all of them have content guidelines—some list of messages, topics, or points of discussion that facilitators could or must use to convey information to parents. Although some content guidelines are overly detailed for the mass audience of parents and facilitators (for example, Ministry of Education and Culture [MoEC]'s 37 booklets), and some content guidelines are missing altogether (for example, *Taman Anak Sejahtera* [TAS]), the majority of programs have reasonable, comprehensive content guidelines. There is no shortage of good information on feeding practices, discipline approaches, stimulating children's social and cognitive development, and so forth. However, existing programs tend to make one of the following errors: They provide no guidance on what key messages to convey, too many messages from which to choose without any focus on a particular goal or set of goals, or no information about how to convey selected messages. Program owners would do well to decide on a narrow set of key messages to convey and state them explicitly for facilitators and parents.

What *is* missing, however, is not general content for parents in general—from which there is abundant information to choose—but specific content for families with specific needs and special problems. There are many groups of at-risk families who would benefit even more than other families from interventions (Hyson & Tomlinson 2014), but we saw no evidence of programs trying to reach out to at-risk families with specific needs (beyond families in poverty and, from Plan, a focus on children with disabilities). Content guidelines are needed for families dealing with: children with disabilities and developmental delays, children with challenging behaviors, abused children or families dealing with domestic violence, families living with chronic stress, children of single-parent families, seasonal and migrant work, incarcerated parents, natural disasters, transition to a new community and culture, a family member with a chronic illness, and so forth. These are all families whose children are at risk for not reaching their potential in terms of health and longevity, cognitive capacities and success, and pyschosocial well-being. There are interventions or relevant content messages available in other countries that could adapted to the Indonesian context.

On the basis of the U.S. Centers for Disease Control and Prevention (CDC) meta-analysis, two content messages that could be enhanced to improve parenting skills might be (1) how to develop good communication skills around emotional development and (2) how to enact effective, nonviolent disciplinary techniques. At present, most programs may touch on but are not strong on emotional communication—teaching parents to name and validate children's emotions and self-regulate (for example, control negative emotions) in safe and constructive ways. This is important because it strengthens children's attachment to parents, increases compliance, and improves both children's *and* parents' well-being. Similarly, most programs do not venture into explaining positive discipline techniques for young children (there are exceptions, such as *Program Keluarga Harapan Family Development Sessions* [PKH/FDS]), but evidence shows that specific skill teaching on how to use positive discipline strategies improves parenting skills.

In short, program developers do not need to develop new parenting programs for the gereral population of parents (including low-income parents), but they could enhance the messages they have by simplifying and better focusing them. Specific populations of at-risk families would also be well served by as-yet-undeveloped interventions tailored to their unique needs. What content facilitators deliver is only half of the story; program designers also need to consider how to strengthen the *way* they deliver that content.

Strengthening Program Design and Delivery

The majority of programs in Indonesia occur for a couple of hours once per month facilitated by an unpaid paraprofessional who may have little more education or experience than the parent participants and typically lacks substantive training or ongoing professional development opportunities. Although there are practical reasons for this type of approach, the evidence suggests it is not a particularly effective way to change parents' attitudes and behaviors, much less to affect children.

Behavior change theorists and researchers tell us that some of the important steps to realizing changes include the following:

- Increasing the sense of self-efficacy so parents believe in themselves and think they can apply a new skill;
- Providing rewards and incentives when necessary;
- Helping parents determine and remember why they are motivated to make behavioral changes;
- Match interventions to parents' stages of awareness;
- Raising awareness through educational materials, confrontation, media campaigns, and individual feedback;
- Include messages that include multiple methods of delivery, are high in emotional content and connect to past experiences;

- Stress the social appropriateness of the desired behavior, and the benefits of that behavior (cf. World Bank, COMMGAP, n.d.).

Incorporating these types of behavioral change agents would likely support the success of program implementation in terms of sustained changes in parents' attitudes and practice.

Several aspects of program design and delivery would probably increase effectiveness if they were implemented or strengthened.

Articulate Goals with a Specific Audience in Mind

At the moment, the majority of parenting programs in Indonesia try to be everything to everyone. They do not cite specific goals but rely on parents and facilitators self direction and fail to follow up on these idiosyncratic goals to see if progress was made. Programs cover an assortment of messages ranging from health and nutrition to positive discipline to money management, and all of the messages are good and important—but parents may not benefit if they are discussed randomly and at a superficial level without follow-up activities. It would be far better to choose a select group of parents with a specific parenting need— say, parents with newborns who need to learn to care for their infants, families who have recently lost a loved one and are grieving, parents of children with disabilities, unemployed parents who want to work, or parents of preschoolers not yet enrolled in school—and articulate goals explicitly aligned with those needs. Even for the more generally applied programs, program designers should target messages and session structure to a specific, rather than universal, audience on characteristics related to socio-economic status (that is, wealth, parental education, employment status) and child status (for example, child age, Early Childhood Development (ECD) or schooling enrollment, transitioning into a program). National providers, local staff, and facilitators should all know who the intended audience is.

Ensure That Goals Are Measurable

In addition to having articulated goals—specific goals for a specific population of parents at a specific "teachable moment" (that is, a time when parents have questions and need extra support)—the goals should be measurable. Often decrees, regulations, and policies express positive messages about the importance of parenting and the need to improve parenting skills without explaining what that actually means. Programs that can state a goal in a way that can be measured are more likely to make progress toward those goals. The following are examples:

- Increased the number of times the parent played with the child (say, per week).
- Increased the number of times the parent spoke words of praise and encouragement to the child.

- Decreased the number of times the parent flicked, hit, yanked, or otherwise physically hurt the child.
- Increased the number of times the parent read, told a story, said a nursery rhyme, or sang to the child.
- Increased the number of fruits and/or vegetables the parent provided to the child.
- Increased the number of hours the child attended playgroup/PAUD/TK.

The actual goals would depend on the needs of the parents in the given program, but the point is that someone—facilitators and parents together—could track these goals and see if any improvements emerged. Facilitators would likely take great pride in seeing the positive results of their efforts through these numbers.

Increase Contact Frequency and Intensity
To see positive results, two hours once per month is probably not enough, especially for at-risk families including parents with low income and education levels. Programs are more likely to see results if they meet weekly or fortnightly and include even more frequent contact between facilitators and parents. Spacing sessions out over several weeks makes sense in practical terms for busy, working, tired parents and facilitators; but it also means lots of time between sessions to forget what was discussed, to fail to apply new skills, to have questions and forget them, and to lose focus on the goals they are trying to achieve. Rather than having 12 sessions over the course of a year, for example, it would be more effective to hold 12 sessions over the course of three to six months, providing a more focused, more intensive effort to change attitudes and behaviors. In addition to parenting group meetings, contacts such as home visits, phone calls, text messages, or Facebook are ways of connecting and maintaining the focus. These contacts could occur between parents as well between facilitators and parents— the point is to have support, encouragement, and accountability. Public service announcements via radio, posters, or billboards would also keep participants (and the community) on message.

Include Opportunity for In-Session Practice with Children
There is no doubt that it is hard to focus on understanding new content, having mature, uninterrupted discussions, and listening attentively with a child in your hands, in your lap, or at your feet—or running across the room. Yet, the evidence is clear that having some time during parenting education sessions for parent-child interaction with feedback is useful and benefits parents and children. While it would perhaps be counter-productive to require children to be present during all the sessions, it would be beneficial to include children for some portions of at least some sessions—as MoEC's emerging grant program for infants and toddlers will do. When facilitators (and other parents) have a chance to observe parents interacting with their infants and young children, they can provide encouragement for the things parents do well and gentle guidance for areas in which they

could improve. Knowledge is only the first level of improving parenting behaviors; application is the higher-level operation. Parents need a chance not only to role play with other adults, but also to practice the new skills about which they are learning with their own children. Being in a supportive environment where parents can watch each other will also deepen their learning and understanding.

Provide Step-by-Step Activity Guidelines for Facilitators

Most program designers and facilitators would say they have guidelines for their programs, but these are often what we call *content guidelines*—lists of topics and constructive messages to impart to parents. How to impart those messages is not explained, however, in most cases (except for in Plan and PKH/FDS modules). A specific set of step-by-step instructions on messages and prescribed activities (for example, small-group discussion, games, role playing, interaction with children, reflection)—what we call *activity guidelines*—can be a big help to facilitators. Given the generally low level of facilitator capacity—some facilitators have higher education but not necessarily in anything related to child development or parenting—a strong degree of structure and support is likely to be more helpful than a vague, open-ended approach to pedagogy. This is also a way to ensure that facilitators use active learning techniques rather than relying on lectures and passive listening. Facilitators should be given ideas and structures for using games, interactive diagolue, self-reflection activities, and role playing, for example, in order to deepen parents' understanding of new ideas and skills. Some might counter that detailing what facilitators should say and what games they should play is rigid and requires the facilitator to act like an expert. While that could be the case, it is more probable that the facilitators sometimes fail in teaching a new point because they do not truly understand it themselves or they do not have ideas for activities to make the teaching interactive. As facilitators gain knowledge and competence with the materials, programs could decide to allow more flexibility in how they present materials and should encourage facilitators to share those ideas with each other. Until they have strong capacity, however, activity guidelines would be a useful tool for facilitators and reduce the pressure on them. It would also make module implementation more uniform and easier to evaluate.

Improve Selection Processes, Training, and Compensation for Facilitators

At present, facilitators in many programs are volunteers, not only in the sense that they work without pay, but also in the sense that they self-nominate to give of their time and energy. There are often no specific selection criteria for skills or personal characteristics, no application and review process (or only a loose and idiosyncratic process), or hiring occurred based on unrelated or tangentially related skills and education. To create an effective program, it is important to select the right people for the job; when program designers create a set of selection criteria, they can then make more informed selection decisions. Criteria should includes both established skills (for example, being bilingual), a willingness to learn new information and skills (for example, knowledge of child development and care, how to promote positive interactions between parents and children), and desirable personal characteristics (for example, empathy, flexibility, humor). The importance of good communication and interpersonal skills cannot be over-emphasized in facilitator selection (Wasik and Bryant 2009).

There is a lot of pressure on facilitators—even in programs philosophically opposed to having facilitators as experts, such as Plan—to come up with either session messages, pedagogy, or both. This should not be the case. Facilitators are perhaps the single most important factor in how effective a program is, and they deserve support so they do not feel pressure but rather feel empowered. A facilitator who is knowledgeable, trusted, supportive, empathic, and skilled in group leadership will run a dynamic and enriching program. A facilitator who lacks those assets still has the potential to do a great job *if* she has great materials to work from—a clear set of messages in a specific sequence and tools for teaching such as videos, illustrations, and activity ideas—*and* excellent training. Training needs to include not only initial training that occurs before the program begins with opportunities to role play and receive feedback, but also ongoing training, such as refresher trainings, multimedia messages and reminders, and coaching from a knowledgeable and supportive supervisor who can convey feedback, advice, and support. Moreover, it is important to find the funds to pay facilitators. Although compensation adds to costs in the present, it will reduce costs in the long run as programs invest in developing competent facilitators who stay in their jobs for a long time, reducing turn-over rates.

Use Written Forms to Collect Standardized Data, Review Results, and Make Improvements

It is hard to compare programs' effectiveness without data, and most programs in Indonesia not only do not evaluate their data but also do not collect it—at least not on the ultimate outcomes, which are parents' knowledge and skills (and children's well-being and success). Most often, programs that collect data focus on facilitators' gains during training, which is important, but not the end goal. (Plan is an exception; facilitators collects data on some parents during home visits, including with parent input.) Many programs do use an informal, discussion-oriented approach to evaluation, wherein facilitators meet, say, monthly to discuss how things are going and how they can improve quality in the next session. However, it is not possible to say with conviction whether a program is working when there is no standardized approach to evaluation and no written component.

Moreover, most of the evaluation that occurs, such as it is, stays at the local level, either within the program itself or at the district level, and ministry or national-level offices do not ask for that data. As a result, NGOs such as World Vision do not know how many parenting programs they run in Indonesia and major governmnet programs such as the MoH *Kelas Ibu* are not quantifiable—staff does not know how many programs there are or where they are, not to mention whether they are effective. Making any noteworthy changes to the programs will require more attention to written data evaluated at the national level—in addition to the already useful conversations at the community level. The national level office has a responsibility to look at the results and determine whether the programs are effective in meeting the named goals. Refinements and improvements, whether in terms of outreach, key messages, or delivery, should be continuous and based on the information provided by the data forms.

Take Better Advantage of Technology

Indonesia is one of the most socially mobile-centric countries in the world: About 60 million mobile phones were sold in the country in 2013 and it is Facebook's fourth-largest market in the world. Indonesians send out over 15 tweets a second (87 percent of which are sent by mobile phone), making Indonesia also the fourth-largest Twitter market in the world, and more Indonesians (96 percent) use social media than read newspapers or listen to the radio. Even among poor Indonesians, the target of many parenting education programs, access to mobile phones and accompanying social media should be a tool in approaches to outreach and contact. Sending sms messages, tweets, Facebook messages, and even making old-fashioned phone calls are a great way to check in with families, have parents report back on their homework, and answer questions mid-week. Messages can be sent to groups or tailored to individuals, making this a flexible, personalized approach. If mobile phone ownership is a barrier to participation, providing a handphone is a relatively inexpensive enticement tool to bring parents into the program or to reward parents for reaching an individual goal. Program designers should be creative in finding ways to make better use of technology.

Although access to computers is lower than access to mobile phones, 65 percent of the population has computer access to the Internet at web cafes or other public places (22 percent have web access at home) (Reed, 2013). In programs such as the PKH/FDS, facilitators have laptops or could access the Internet to watch refresher training videos, get new reading materials, or contact each other for ideas and support. World Vision and recently Plan have made their modules available to facilitators on a centralized site, making distribution of materials far simpler than relying on hard copy publications alone. In what will surely be the most widely used parenting education application, the likely new directorate for parenting education at MoEC is creating an interactive website for parents to dispense curricular information, advice, and techniques to support child development and learning. As described, the website has potential to serve as an excellent toolkit for parents and facilitators alike. These and other inexpensive applications of technology can be ideal in this highly tech-friendly country, and has potential to reach rural and remote areas, facilitators in all areas, and families, whether served by parenting programs or not.

Strengthening the System

The aforementioned suggestions are generally useful for strengthening individual programs. Here, we highlight five ways to strengthen the system as a whole, followed by 10 steps that should be enacted for optimal implementation of a strong system.

Name a Lead Agency But Use the Expertise and Delivery Mechanisms of All Relevant Program Providers

Because the early years belong to a wide array of fields—health, education, psychology, child protection, family welfare, parenting programs, community programs, and so forth—it can ironically get lost in the shuffle, as noted earlier. This is especially true in a country like Indonesia where not only are multiple sectors involved, but also decentralization requires that every province and district be involved. Just as there are great efforts to coordinate efforts on behalf of children's holistic, integrated ECD program experiences, a body or agency dedicated to coordinating the many parenting education programs could help prevent certain groups of parents from being overlooked and underserved.

Naming a lead agency would *not* mean deferring all parenting education decisions or programing efforts to that agency. Rather, it would mean:

- Strengthening that agency's capacities at the district level, ensuring an active office in every district;
- Equipping the agency to do ongoing needs assessment in each community to determine family's needs and government and program goals in that area; and
- Allowing the agency to work with relevant ministries per the results of the needs assessment.

Each ministry has important expertise and deliverty platforms to offer. Should the need in a given community be, say, to decrease stunting, the lead agency and MoH could work together to implement a program with feeding and nutrition content; should the goal be to better integrate special needs children into schools and communities, the lead agency and Ministry of Social Affairs (MoSA) could work together to increase awareness and decrease stigmatization; should the goal be to increase school readiness skills, the lead agency and MoEC could implement a program highlighting child stimulation practices, logistical information about local preprimary programs, and the importance of language skills; and so forth. The importance of using existing expertise and mechanisms cannot be overstated, because of the holistic nature of children's development and family's needs—and due to Indonesia's progress in promoting Holistic, Integrated Early Childhood Development (HI-ECD).

In addition to granting oversight to a lead agency to determine the needs for parenting support, an entity such as *Pemberdayaan Kesejahteraan Keluarga* (PKK), the district-level organization responsible for women's and families' well-being—might be a useful mechanism for community mobilization on parenting education. Strengthening PKK as a supporting agency to both understand parents' needs and increase outreach to all parents could enhance parenting activities and impact program outcomes.

Conduct or Commission Research on Parenting in Indonesia

To make solid, evidence-based recommendations on improving parenting education programs in Indonesia, research is needed on parenting in Indonesia. In a
country as diverse and culturally rich as this one, research by region would be
most revealing and informative for developing programs, both in terms of building on families' and communities' strengths, and to build up areas of weakness,
where there are widespread gaps in knowledge or skills, whether about nutrition
and health knowledge, about school readiness and the importance of preschool,
or about ways to support children and families in times of disaster. Indonesia has
a fundamental flaw in its foundation until more data are available about what
parents believe, what they know, what they want to know, how their behavior
influences their children's well-being and success, and where differences lie
between groups of parents. The World Bank Impact Evaluation provides an
example of the type of data that would help shape programs.

Ensure That Parenting Program Measures Are Performance Indicators

Many programs and offices at every level of participation believe that parents
are critical to children's well-being and success, yet they rarely quantify those
beliefs as performance indicators. Until relevant ministries make parenting program measures items on their performance-indicator list, parenting is likely to
be overlooked and underfunded. Each ministry should contribute to improving
children's well-being according to its own area of expertise, but all areas can be
enhanced by working with parents and each ministry should consider how it can
best work with parents to support children and families and create or strength-
en parenting programs to do so. Performance indicators are basic component of
monitoring program effectiveness. Once minisitries are required to show how
they fare in terms of quality of and enrollment in parenting programs, they will
have greater incentive to create and enhance programs, invest in materials, training, and retaining a qualified workforce, and tracking parents' outcomes (and
children's). It will ensure that planning documents (for example, the long-term
plan for Bappenas) include parenting indicators. Programs that do well are
likely to see increased funding for their good performance, creating a virtuous
cycle. In addition to focusing attention on parenting education in a stronger way,
having performance indicators at the national level will prompt officials to
ensure that districts keep track of their data as well, which is critical for program
improvement.

Make Parenting Education Available to All Parents According to Need, Not Only to Parents Using ECD Programs

Kindergarten, playgroup, day care, and other ECD programs can provide an
excellent entry point to reaching families with parenting support services.
However, systems for enhancing and increasing parenting education opportunities should be considered separately from children's early childhood education
experiences for at least two reasons. First, parents have different needs and

different approaches to learning than do children, and early childhood educators may not be the best people to teach adults, either because they do not know the full range of necessary content or may not have the comfort level and leadership skills necessary to teach adults. Second, a focus only on parents of children already enrolled in ECD programs would leave out many underserved parents, such as parents of infants and toddlers, children with disabilities, children with challenging behaviors, children dealing with domestic violence or natural disasters, and so forth. ECD and parenting programs are extremely well-suited to working together because of the overlap in required knowledge of child development and care, but participation in one should not require participation in the other, and performance indicators should be tracked separately so that both types of programs get the intellectual and financial attention they deserve.

MoEC, especially with its new directorate for parenting education, could take a leadership role in programs designed to help parents understand the importance of ECD program enrollment, know how to strengthen their children's language and literacy skills, learn how to improve children's self-regulation and social skills so they are ready for school, and support children's success once they are in school. Ministries with expertise on child safety, health and nutrition, parent-child interactions, sibling rivalry, dealing with divorce, death, or crises, child or adult mental health issues, and so forth would be in a better position than MoEC to take the lead on providing parenting education on those given topics. Because many parents do not use early childhood education programs and because MoEC's role focuses on educational success specifically, it is important not to put the burden on MoEC to address all issues for all parents.

Create Standards for Parenting Education Programs

One possible approach that the government of Indonesia might take to ensure that all parents have access to parenting education programs and that all parenting education programs are of good quality is to create standards for parenting education programs. Such standards would align with existing child outcome standards used by education programs, but would not be limited to those standards, which would not all be relevant for all parenting programs; parenting program goals will be variable according to the needs of the community and should be narrowly focused on a specific set of improvements in parents' knowledge or skills, rather than trying to improve all outcomes for all children of all ages. Parenting education program standards could set goals for content, pedagogy, and program structure (for example, facilitators use active learning techniques, key messages are closely aligned with the goals and specific needs of the families, facilitators have content and activity guidelines, facilitators receive initial and ongoing training). How program organizers choose to meet those standards would vary, allowing for flexibility according to local culture, language, availability and quality of facilitators, and characteristics and needs of parents and families (see table 5.1).

Table 5.1 Indonesia Parenting Education System: Matrix of Recommended Actions

Short-term (within 2 years)	Time (years)	Medium-term (3–5 years)	Time (years)
1. Develop the framework			
Reach consensus on lead agency that will provide oversight and coordination.	1	None	None
Develop and disseminate parenting education program standards.	1–2	None	None
Reach consensus on a discrete set of national goals for parenting education.	2	None	None
Task relevant ministries and NGOs with adapting or developing programs that align with district needs and national goals.	2	None	None
2. Create an enabling environment			
Leverage existing platforms of community engagement to incentivize experimentation at the community level to add or improve parenting education programs.	Initiate in year 1 and sustain	None	None
Increase demand for parenting education programs using public relations campaigns, parent outreach, and social media.	Initiate in year 1 and sustain	None	None
3. Conduct the research			
Conduct needs assessments at the district level on service delivery gaps for parenting education programs.	1	Reevaluate districts' needs as necessary.	3–5
Determine gaps in the knowledge base about parenting practices and outcomes within diverse cultural, socioeconomic, and disadvantaged groups in Indonesia; conduct studies to close these gaps and inform design of improved programs.	1–2	Continue the research programs.	3–5
Develop core materials for parenting education programs in light of research findings.	2	Pilot core materials.	3–4

table continues next page

Table 5.1 Indonesia Parenting Education System: Matrix of Recommended Actions *(continued)*

Short-term (within 2 years)	Time (years)	Medium-term (3–5 years)	Time (years)
Develop training procedure for facilitators of parenting education programs.	2	Pilot training for facilitators.	3–4
Engage M&E experts to inform the development of indicators and rigorous study designs to evaluate the effectiveness of these new parenting education programs.	Initiate in year 1 and sustain	Ensure M&E experts continue to participate in analyzing and using research results to refine program content and delivery.	3–5
4. Implement and refine programing			
Develop monitoring mechanisms to ensure data are compiled, analyzed, and used to make program improvements.	Initiate in year 1 and sustain	Refine parenting education programs on the basis of lessons from monitoring.	Initiate in year 3 and sustain
Train Master Trainers using existing training facilities and institutions.	2	Hire and train facilitators to implement the respective programs. Ensure continuous professional development opportunities for facilitators.	Initiate in year 3 and sustain
Plan expanded implementation strategies to ensure access to all target families.	2	Scale up effective programs to increase coverage and reach appropriate target families.	Initiate in year 4 and sustain
		Compare progress against national goals and revise strategies accordingly.	Initiate in year 4 and sustain

Note: M&E = Monitoring and evaluation; NGO = nongovernmental organization.

Steps to Get from Here to There

What has been described is a sense of what would be ideal for parenting education in Indonesia. As mentioned at the start of the study, the process is in early days. The following is a suggested sequence of steps, some of which can occur simultaneously:

1. Relevant stakeholders at the national level come to consensus on which is the best agency to lead and coordinate parenting education programs, regardless of desired outcomes or delivery methods.
2. A list of the glaring gaps in knowledge about parenting in Indonesia is determined by scholars and academics. Initiatives to conduct research on parenting practices are implemented throughout Indonesia, with specific attention to various types of vulnerable families, not only poor versus nonpoor, as well as regional differences.

3. Relevant stakeholders meet to finalize a list of goals at the national level they would like to address through parenting education programs.
4. The lead agency bolsters support for district level agencies and together national and district offices conduct needs assessments throughout the districts to gather district-level information on parenting attitudes, knowledge, and skills. The data are compiled and evaluated at the national level.
5. Parenting education program standards are established and agreed upon such that, regardless of desired outcomes or delivery methods, there is a quality benchmark each program should strive to achieve.
6. After determining the salient needs across districts, the lead agency identifies appropriate ministries or NGOs to design parenting education programs on specific topics and for specific audiences, either by using existing effective programs or by building new modules, making sure to create content and activity guidelines for facilitators.
7. Involved agencies hire and train a sufficient number of facilitators who have the relevant qualifications and characteristics to effectively implement the program. Facilitators receive both preservice and ongoing training using existing training agencies and institutions wherever possible, and providean adequate compensation that goes beyond transportation reimbursement, in order to reduce turnover.
8. PKK, district offices, and the national lead agency work together to increase demand for parenting education programs among parents and communities, through public relations campaigns, parent outreach programs, and informational bulletins on social media.
9. Programs are implemented by the various responsible ministries and NGOs. Monitoring and evaluation (M&E) data inform continuous improvements to the programs, while the national lead agency provides feedback systems to all participating ministries and agencies and ensures targets are being met and no vulnerable families are going unserved.
10. An M&E agency independent of the lead agency is named and tasked with designing a system to capture baseline and endline data, and to analyze results and make recommendations for improvements.

In Closing

In closing, Indonesia has many excellent tools and models at its fingertips. There is no reason to "reinvent the wheel" by developing new programs for the general population. Rather, enhancing the existing programs according to their respective merits and creating programs for un-served populations of families with specific needs would be useful. There is no need to favor a particular model over other models because the programs reach various audiences of parents and do so in various ways, which is generally beneficial. The needs are rather to (1) improve programs where they are lacking; (2) make sure program content and structure matches the needs of the parents; and

(3) create new programs for unreached parents, both those families in remote or un-served areas (using existing high-quality parenting programs) and those families with specific needs that are not yet addressed by current programs (using not-yet-created programs).

Indonesia will benefit tremendously by investing in parents of young children, both in human terms and economic terms. As vulnerable as young children are, it is important to remember that parents are vulnerable too. We need to value parents not merely as conduits to reaching children, but as worthy of attention, support, and admiration in their own right. Whether poor or rich, unschooled or well-educated, being a new parent is a daunting prospect. The programs outlined in this study all contribute tremendously to enriching and empowering parents to lead lives of greater value, contribution, and joy as they deepen their positive experiences of parenting.

Parenting Education in Indonesia: Seven Program Examples from the Field

Ministry of Health (MoH)'s *Kelas Ibu*

Overview

The national MoH office is the origin of two parenting education classes provided to mothers in all 33 provinces across the county: *Kelas Ibu Hamil* (classes for pregnant women) and *Kelas Ibu Balita* (classes for mothers of children younger than five years of age), collectively referred to as *Kelas Ibu* or Mother Classes.

Location

District health offices must offer these classes to community residents, with initial contact with women primarily through *posyandu* (village health post providing integrated services) and *puskesmas* (health center usually serving several villages).

Content
- Mother Classes are usually once per month and last 1–1.5 hours.
- Classes typically consist of about 10–15 mothers, and bigger groups are separated by mothers of younger versus older children within the birth to age 5 range. Children may or may not be present during the class; class design does not presume or require children's presence.
- A primary objective of the *Kelas Ibu* program is to increase parents' use of the maternal and child health (MCH) handbook, often referred to as "the pink book." It contains practical tips and important guidance on pregnancy, delivery, post-partum mother and baby care, immunization requirements, breastfeeding and nutritious foods across the early years, common illnesses, and benchmarks for child growth and development.

Facilitators

The two most common types of MoH Mother Class facilitators are midwives and paraprofessional women in the community, called *kaders*. They serve as facilitators on a volunteer basis, without financial incentives or other compensation.

Coverage

The primary means of evaluating the success and reach of the program is by keeping track of how many MCH booklets are printed each year. National MoH staff estimates how many mothers in Indonesia will give birth in the coming year, then prints enough pink books for 80 percent of that estimated total. On the basis of that formula, the office planned to print 4.7 million MCH books in 2014.

Box A.1   Ministry of Health Collaboration with the Global Maternal and Child Health Integrated Program (MCHIP)

The U. S. Agency for International Development (USAID) initiated a global maternal and child health program in 2009, called the Maternal and Child Health Integrated Program (MCHIP). It brought Indonesia into the MCHIP mechanism for a three-year program from January 2010 to December 2012, which had a considerable impact on how the Ministry of Health (MoH) now implements its *kelas ibu* program nationally.

Participants

Three remote districts classified as "health problem areas," participated in the program: Serang in the Banten Province, Kutai Timur District in East Kalimantan, and Bireuen in Aceh. MCHIP organizers expanded the eligible participant circle to include lactating or post-partum women as well.

Costs and Contributions

Mothers generally do not pay for class participation. In the new agreement with private hospitals, parents, at least in the Jakarta area, will pay approximately Rp 50,000 per class. USAID funded the overall Indonesia program with a budget of USD 9.8 million, which covered strengthening services for hospitals and *puskesmas* as well as aspects more directly related to mother classes.

Content of MCHIP Activity

Home visits—MCHIP staff and partners created a schedule for home visits and adopted global guidelines to the Indonesian context for use with midwives. Staff also adapted a checklist of tasks for care by midwives, developed according to child age.

Mother classes—Although *kaders* or midwives may serve as class facilitators in the overall national program, MCHIP program organizers trained only *kaders* to serve as class facilitators for the classes in their project districts. They trained village midwives to supervise *kaders*. A second layer of supervision existed from *puskesmas* personnel, who monitored both *kader* and midwife performance.

Revision of MoH materials—With MCHIP input, MoH updated their facilitator guidelines to reflect the wider audience of participating mothers by including content for women who had recently had a baby. They also revised materials for use with *kaders* rather than midwives; to include self-tests for knowledge assessment before and after class participation; to have larger and clearer illustrations; and by adding a flipchart to help the learning of both facilitators and mothers.

box continues next page

Box A.1 Ministry of Health Collaboration with the Global Maternal and Child Health Integrated Program (MCHIP) *(continued)*

Mini-university—Using province-level health offices as the focal point, mini-universities served as information sessions for more than 650 government personnel at national, province, and district levels held in classroom-type settings. Organizers successfully used the sessions (six classes) to explain the accomplishments of MCHIP.

Results

MCHIP facilitated 238 classes across 139 villages in the 3 districts. The classes reached over 12,000 mothers and pregnant women. In terms of home visits in the week after birth, rates rose from 72 percent in 2010 to 87 percent in 2012. By district, rates rose as follows: in Bireuen, from 85 percent to 98 percent; in Serang, from 77 percent to 98 percent; and in Kutai Timur, from 55 percent to 65 percent.

Overall, program organizers found that data collection systems were weak. They noted two particular challenges: limited capacity within district health offices and *puskesmas* to monitor data quality and confusion on the part of midwives regarding the indicators on which they are meant to collect data. Program organizers instituted monthly meetings for *puskesmas* personnel to strengthen data collection processes.

In summary, although the MCHIP program only operated in three districts, it had a significant impact on MoH sessions and materials by expanding parenting education to women with infants, a critical time for teaching and learning new attitudes and practices that affect infant health and well-being—not only in physical ways, but also in social, emotional, and cognitive ways as mothers bond with and better understand and enjoy their babies.

Financing
Unavailable.

Strengths
The MoH program undoubtedly has an excellent platform for reaching a vast number of families with young children, especially low- and moderate-income families. Every district has a *posyandu*, through which *Kelas Ibu* can be offered (although some remote areas still lack even a basic health clinic; and some well-off parents choose private clinics). This is a major strength of the program.

Recommendations
- Strengthen linkages with health facilities since all mothers seek health services but not educational services.
- Make Mother Classes mandatory for parents of young children in addition to pregnant women.
- Emphasize the importance of psychosocial benefits of good health habits in Mother Classes.
- Reach out to fathers to involve them in supporting and caring for mothers, infants, and young children.
- Make training tailored for the type of facilitator.

National Board on Family Planning (BKKBN)'s BKB Program

Overview

Government guidelines convey authority for implementing holistic, integrated Early Childhood Development (ECD) programs (*Pedoman Umum PAUDHI*) and for overseeing parenting education programs to BKKBN. BKKBN offers parenting classes called *Bina Keluarga Balita* (BKB, Building Families of Young Children Groups), reaching parents in most districts and providing comprehensive content and messages that reflect all domains of child development in age-specific ways.

Location

Parents may be invited through interactions with *posyandu* services or ECD (playgroup or PAUD) services. Often the sessions occur at the playgroup or PAUD center during children's class time, when parents (typically mothers) have time to participate.

Content

- Parents meet on a monthly, bi-monthly, or weekly basis, depending on the BKB group.
- The "BKB kit" includes materials such as:
  - BKB guidelines: facilitator guidebook that discusses facilitators' role and how to conduct parent meetings.
  - Information on parents' role in children's growth and development, development of young children, parent-child interactions, and basic needs for women in the pregnant and post-partum periods.
  - Child Development Chart (KKA): a graph following various child development domains.
  - Discussion cards, flipcharts, posters, toys for facilitators to conduct the BKB.
- BKB is frequently coordinated or integrated with PAUD programs (playgroups, day care centers, kindergartens) and *posyandu* services.

Facilitators

Facilitators are usually women invited by community leaders to be BKB *kaders* because of their experience with working with young children; they may or may not be working in other roles while also serving as a BKB *kader*. They may receive some reimbursement for travel costs but are otherwise unpaid volunteers. For each five to six villages in rural areas (or one to two communities in cities like Jakarta), there is a supervisor who provides support to the *kaders*. Supervisors may be government employees or others. Government officials are paid for their supervisory work commensurate with their pay grade.

Box A.2 Snapshot of a High-Quality BKB Program

We observed an integrated PAUD-BKB-*posyandu* during a field visit to a BKB class in sub-district of Sewan in the Yogyakarta area in February 2013. Staff included six PAUD teachers and 10 BKB *kaders*. *Kaders* had received an integrated training from the Ministry of National Development Planning (Bappenas), with BKB, *posyandu*, and PAUD staff in the same room.

The agenda for BKB parenting sessions was generally an opening speech and prayer, followed by a review of the previous topic, followed by discussion of a new topic. Parents were grouped according to their child's age—so there were three groups meeting in three areas of the center—but each group discussed the same topic as predetermined by the *kaders* (for example, interesting toys and activities for children). *Kaders* distributed a *kantong wasiat* (card pulled from a cloth pouch hanging on the wall) to each parent, which one of the parents read aloud. Cards are developed by the national-level BKKBN office. The *kader* then explained the information presented on the card in more detail or added to it. If so directed by the card, the *kader* and parents practiced an activity together. This was followed by sharing personal stories and examples and a question and answer time. *Kaders* noted that sometimes they make cookies, jewelry or handicrafts during the sessions. We also observed one of the *kaders* showing a short video to her group about helping and including children with disabilities.

Coverage

There are 85,884 BKB programs and 3.7 million member families with children younger than five years of age. Therefore, each BKB group has on average 44 member families—although not all members participate in the parenting classes. In a BKKBN survey (2012) using systematic random sampling of over 44,000 member households, they found that approximately 32 percent (13,500) were families with young children. Of these, 16 percent (2,100) of parents participated in BKB classes in the previous three months, lower than BKKBN expected.

Financing

Annual budget of Rp 5.3 billion.

Strengths

Planners have designed the delivery of the program well; it has good interactive components that work with parents' strengths. Parents discuss selected topics, role play, problem solve, and actively engage with each other. BKB is uniquely positioned to integrate both education and health program components through its collaboration with PAUD and *posyandu*.

Recommendations

On the basis of a third-party review of the BKB as well as our research, we recommend the following:

- Simplify the materials in the BKB kit, making them shorter and more easily understood by *kaders* and parents.
- Make efforts to retain *kaders* and reduce turnover (currently at 70 percent) in order to improve program unity and institutional knowledge.
- Increase the frequency of classes to twice a month (now typically once per month).
- Continue to emphasize the whole child approach, showing parents how they can help their children develop and learn by focusing not just on physical development, but also on how children play, learn, speak, and behave.
- Emphasize an integrated approach (both education and health programs).
- Given the known link between practice and feedback opportunities and improved parent and child behaviors, build a mother-child interactive component into the program. Sessions are often held in conjunction with PAUD programs—that is, while mothers attend the parenting class, children attend center-based care at the same location—which means that the BKB program design easily offers the opportunity for parent-child interaction during sessions.
- Tailor messages and sessions to parents with children entering PAUD or entering school, in order to help ease the transition for both parents and children.

Box A.3 Development of New Materials

At the request of BKKBN, United Nations Children's Fund (UNICEF) is creating a set of seven booklets for use with parents who are BKB participants. The hope is that the booklets will equip parents with useful parenting tools so they can apply better parenting skills. Developers hope the booklets could be adapted and used by other ministries in the future. UNICEF further suggested that a multimedia approach could be very successful, involving posters, stickers, leaflets, television public announcements, and videos. The program will be jointly funded by UNICEF and BKKBN over a five-year period (2013–18).

In addition, BKKBN has recently developed a new book called *"Orangtua Pintar,"* or "Being a Smart Parent," for distribution to parents. It is not clear how BKKBN plans to deliver and use this book in relation to the seven booklets just described. The book discusses how to build effective communication with children and how to handle misbehavior without punishment. It does not have accompanying facilitator materials or plans for training.

Ministry of Education and Culture (MoEC)'s Grant Programs

Overview
In 2013, the ministry had implemented or planned to implement parenting education through two grant programs: (1) grants for all parents of children ages zero to six and (2) grants for only parents of children ages zero to three.[1] MoEC provides these grants to existing ECD programs that submit successful proposals to be used towards creating a parenting education program for parents. Oversight of the grant money is the responsibility of the recipient school or a program management committee (often consisting of parents, school administrators, and village members). In 2015, MoEC is exploring the possibility of establishing a General Directorate of Parenting Education.

Location
MoEC's parenting education grants target parents of children already enrolled in an ECD program. All types of ECD programs are included, such as kindergartens, playgroups, and other PAUD programs.

Content
There are three strategies for teaching and engaging with parents:

- Parenting classes: Usually takes place once per month and lasts no more than two hours, with both mothers and fathers encouraged to come. The arrangement and content of the parenting classes are decided collectively by the group and not standardized by MoEC staff. MoEC prints a collection of 37 books that may be used as materials and background reading for facilitators to use for parenting classes.
- "Parents' Days:" MoEC encourages programs to increase parents' involvement in children's learning by having parents participate in children's ECD programs. Participation could be that a parent comes in to the classroom to demonstrate an activity, teach a new skill, tell stories, or help celebrate a holiday.
- Home visits: Teachers have a chance to talk privately with parents. In most cases, home visits occur because a teacher has a concern about a child.

In addition to these three strategies, the grants targeted for only parents of children ages zero to three requires hands-on activities for parents to play and care for their child during the parenting education sessions.

Facilitators
Facilitators are usually health personnel, religious leaders, or ECD teachers. There is no training required of facilitators.

Coverage
The coverage of this program is extremely small, since only one center per province receives a grant. In 2013, the first year of implementation, MoEC provided

grants to 25 ECD programs (one per province) to provide parenting classes for one year. In 2014, MoEC is providing one grant for each of the 33 provinces.

Financing
Each grant recipient receives Rp 25 million per year. MoEC budgets an additional Rp 3.3 billion per year, which is allocated for workshops and capacity building for parenting education programs.

Strengths
MoEC's involvement in parenting education is significant in two ways. First, it shows that the government recognizes the critical importance of education for children at their earliest stages. Second, MoEC is uniquely positioned to ensure every child in every district and village has access to education, given its role in managing the basic education system. One of the aspects of MoEC's approach that should be heavily underscored and applauded is the requirement that parents interact with their infants and toddlers in the emerging program.

Recommendations
- Clearly identify goals of the grant program in terms of parenting behaviors and attitudes or child outcomes.
- Develop a set of guidelines or standardized curriculum for facilitators to use in order to ensure that parents receive helpful, correct information.
- Ensure that ECD centers have equal opportunity to submit successful grant proposals, either through a blind review process or by offering special support for weaker programs.

Ministry of Social Affairs (MoSA)'s TAS and PKH/FDS Programs

Overview
The Ministry of Social Affairs (MoSA) has two parenting education programs, each under different directorates. The first is *Taman Anak Sejahtera* (TAS), which provides parenting education grants to at-risk children that are part of the ministry's social welfare program, *Program Kesejahteraan Sosial Anak* (PKSA). The second is *Program Keluarga Harapan* (PKH), a conditional cash transfer system in which parents of poor households receive payments for participating in certain health and education activities. Parenting education classes are part of the Family Development Session (FDS), which is offered under the PKH.

Location
- TAS: Funds are provided to ECD centers. Social workers at the district level choose at-risk children in these ECD centers who would benefit from additional support through the TAS funds.
- PKH/FDS: PKH identifies chronically or very poor households, which are expected to attend monthly meetings where FDS parenting education ses-

sions are offered along with other administrative health and education activities. These meetings typically occur in either a parent's or facilitator's home.

Content
- TAS: Facilitators work together with the selected children's parents to decide how to spend the TAS funds to best support their children. One of the ways staff may decide to spend the money is on the parenting education sessions. However, there are no guidelines for implementing such sessions.
- PKH/FDS: FDS sessions cover a range of topic including health and nutrition, child protection, financial literacy, and parenting skills to support children's social-emotional and cognitive development. The parenting education part of the FDS session covers four content areas: (1) good parenting, (2) understanding children's behavior, (3) playing and learning go together, and (4) success in schools.

Facilitators
- TAS: Facilitators, called *sakti pekerja social*, are social workers paid by MOSA under the Children's Welfare Directorate to support the PKSA (Children's Social Welfare Program), where TAS is part of it.
- PKH/FDS: FDS facilitators are current PKH employees, who are hired through a competitive application process and paid by PKH district offices (monthly salary of approximately Rp 2.3 million). FDS Facilitators are required to have at least a D3 diploma, which is equivalent to about three years of college, and receive four to six days of basic training regarding PKH operations. In addition, there are MoSA-employed Master Trainers who train the FDS facilitators.

Coverage
- TAS: In 2013, 650 TAS facilitators served 8,000 children ages zero to five across 22 provinces. Providers do not know how many parents from that population received parenting education services specifically.
- PKH/FDS: The PKH program currently reaches 3 million poor families across the country. By early 2015, 433 facilitators had received training to implement the modules in 122 sub-districts across 3 provinces: DKI Jakarta, Jawa Barat, and Jawa Timur.

Financing
- TAS: Annual budget of Rp 1.5 million per child to implement parenting education plus annual operational budget of Rp 100,000 per child for fulfilling child's basic needs (could opt to use for parenting education).
- PKH/FDS: Mothers participating in the PKH program receive cash payments from the Government receive between IDR 600,000 and IDR 2,200,000 (US$45–$167) per year for their participation in the program, depending on location, number of children, and activities. In addition to its budget for paying mothers directly, each district-level PKH secretariat has a

budget for operations. From this budget, facilitators receive small amounts of money to purchase stationery or make copies of materials—although the parenting education sessions per se are not expected to incur any operational costs to the district.

Box A.4 In-Depth Look at the PKH/FDS Content for Parenting Education Sessions

Module 1: Good Parenting

Key Message 1 is about positive self-image and parents as role models. Discussion points include: Parents are children's most powerful role models for values and behavior; being poor financially does not mean being poor as parents; good parents are loving, consistent, and not often angry; and having positive beliefs about being parents leads to benefits to children and parents. Key Message 2 is about fathers' role and parenting as a team. Discussion points include: the importance of fathers as caregivers; being united as parents; keeping conflict away from children; and benefits to children and parents.

Module 2: Understanding Children's Behavior

Key Message 1 is about increasing children's good behavior. Discussion topics include: using praise and appreciation to increase good behavior, using tangible rewards for positive behavior, acknowledging children's unique gifts and strengths, and benefits to children and parents. Key Message 2 is about decreasing children's bad behavior—a frequently noted concern among PKH parents. Facilitators will discuss the importance of the 3 Ks (*komitmen, konsekuensi,* and *konsistensi* or commitment, consequences, and consistency; rule setting, planned ignoring, using time outs; not using physical punishment (a common approach); and the benefits of these approaches for children and parents.

Module 3: Playing and Learning Go Together

Key Message 1 is about playing and learning at home. Discussion will include the importance of play for young children; how to support play at different ages; building play into families' daily routines; and the benefits of play for children and parents. Key Message 2 is about the many languages of children: the languages children use, hearing and speaking the mother tongue, early steps toward reading and writing, storytelling, and the benefits to children and parents.

Module 4: Success in School

Key Message 1 is about playing and learning at preschool. Facilitators will explain that good preschool programs use play to help children learn; what children learn in preschool; the location, hours, and costs of nearby preschool options; and the benefits of preschool participation for children and parents. The second Key Message focuses on how to help children succeed in school. Talking points include discussion of good homework practices and parents' provision of time, space, and help; praising children's accomplishments and effort at school; knowing and talking with children's teachers; children's right to education and the importance of not missing school for work; overcoming children's resistance to school; and the benefits to children and parents of achievement at school.

Box A.5 Impact Evaluation of PKH/FDS

MoSA coordinated with the National Development Planning Agency (Bappenas) and the World Bank to design monitoring and evaluation plans, using a randomized control trial approach. Researchers are collecting data on 122 *kecamatan* (subdistricts) implementing the treatment (that is, PKH/FDS modules) and 122 *kecamatan* serving as control groups. They will begin analyzing data in early 2016.

Strengths
- MoSA's programs have the potential to reach a huge number of families most in need of parenting information in Indonesia: chronically poor families who lack not only financial resources, but also social and knowledge resources.
- The PKH/FDS modules have strong program content, addressing multiple important concepts across children's health, social-emotional, and cognitive domains, as well as structured activity guidelines that should raise the quality of program implementation

Recommendations
- TAS: Program providers need to articulate goals and target audiences, then provide content and activity guidelines for facilitators. Providers should track progress toward the selected indicators.
- PKH: The PKH/FDS program aims to tackle a very wide range of knowledge and skills, ranging from household budget management to child discipline and success in school. It may be more effective to narrow the goal set and provide more intensive training on smaller amounts of material.
- PKH: Providers should ensure that FDS facilitators, who already have full-time jobs managing the operations of PKH, are not stretched too thin. Hiring facilitators with more targeted qualifications and training who are available to meet once per week with this less-educated population of parents would likely lead to better results. Providers could also consider dedicating two focal persons at MoSA entirely to FDS implementation, per the recommendations of pilot project evaluators.

Plan Indonesia's Kelompok Pengasuhan Anak (KPA)

Overview
Plan is an international humanitarian, child-centered organization without any religious or governmental affiliation. Plan Indonesia offers two types of parenting groups: (1) classes for pregnant women and peer support groups for lactating mothers, and (2) *Kelompok Pengasuhan Anak* (KPA), which are parenting groups to improve parenting practices related to early stimulation.

Location

Plan Indonesia implements holistic and integrated services for early childhood primarily through the *posyandu* (village health post providing integrated services), but groups also sometimes meet at PAUD centers, community centers, and other venues.

Content of KPA Groups

- Meets monthly to cover 10 sessions of parenting education. Sessions usually last two hours.
- Group size is 15–30 participants. Participants are primarily mothers, who often bring their young children. Staff requires that facilitators ask mothers to invite fathers, who sometimes come as well.
- Facilitators run highly reflective and interactive sessions using a three-step process. First, they raise parents awareness of children's rights. Second, they teach skills and activities to promote children's early stimulation, growth, and development. Third, they encourage parents to initiate collective actions in their community to support children's well-being and development.
- Facilitators receive general guidelines for leading parenting groups called *Strengthening Families for Better Early Childhood Outcomes: A Parenting Education Curriculum Guide.*
- Facilitators conduct or encourage two supplementary components beyond the core sessions:
  - Home visits: Typically after each session, a kader makes unannounced visits to 5 out of the approximately 15 participants.
  - Community Action Plans: At the end of the 10 sessions, facilitators encourage parents to meet for an extra session to discuss issues related to child well-being that requires a collective action plan. Groups have decided on a range of creative plans to better the community for children: to build a latrine for a house, plant fruit trees, conduct a cleanup of the environment, address water storage, create a buddy system for older children to help younger children transition to primary school, or adopt a village-wide homework time for all children.

Facilitators

Facilitators typically are *posyandu kaders* or sometimes parent volunteers or village midwives. Volunteers receive training from Plan staff on *posyandu* information systems, facilitation skills for group sessions, and general health, child protection, and parenting skills. Additional training is provided for health workers on topics such as exclusive breastfeeding, and village midwives receive training on the skills needed for successful deliveries and management and referral of complications for women, newborns, and young children. Facilitators are trained not to dominate sessions and not to implement session guidelines strictly, but rather to remain flexible and inclusive of parents. Facilitators are not paid but receive compensation for travel costs.

Box A.6 Strengthening Families for Better Early Childhood Outcomes: A Parenting Education Curriculum Guide

While the content and delivery of parenting sessions can vary by group, the facilitator guidebook, *Strengthening Families for Better Early Childhood Outcomes: A Parenting Education Curriculum Guide*, contains four modules:

A. Stage 1 Modules: Establishing baseline
B. Stage 2 Modules: Parenting basics
C. Stage 3 Modules: Using pictorial tools to monitor and stimulate child development
D. Stage 4 Modules: What did we learn and what do we want to do next?

For each module, facilitators can read about the purpose of the session and desired participant outcomes and consider background reading materials. Participant outcomes for a session on child protection are, for example, for participants to talk to the spouse and neighbors about the parenting group session; to be able to describe what it means for a child to be safe and protected; to learn at least one strategy from parenting group members for addressing safety concerns; and so forth. The guidelines provide steps facilitators could follow in the session, such as a welcome period, going over the purpose, a review of the previous session, a time to discuss new knowledge and practices, group work, modeling a new practice, wrap up, assignment for home, and selecting a parent volunteer to co-lead in the following session.

Plan uses a cascade training approach, providing Training of Trainers at the district level. Organizers encourage *kaders* to co-facilitate with Plan staff. After a co-facilitation experience—that is, co-leading a 10-session parenting group—these *kaders* receive training as well. *Kaders* then continued to serve as the sole facilitators with new batches of parents. Plan staff ongoing supervision and support.

Coverage

134 groups operate across 3 districts in Nusa Tenggara Timur [NTT] (82 KPA in Sikka; 44 in Lembata; and 8 in Kefamenanu), serving 54 poor villages. Of these, external reviewers rated 79 out of 85 pilot programs as effective, meaning they met regularly, held in-depth discussions focused on child well-being; and provided practice opportunities and outreach. Plan reported that between July 2012 and June 2013, 2,521 parents/caregivers participated in Plan Indonesia's 207 parenting programs.

Financing

Plan Indonesia receives funding from multiple sources to support its work related to parenting education. In 2013, Plan reported that Australia Aid (now the Department of Foreign Affairs and Trade) and Plan Australia provided US$59,000 per year, Plan US provided US$65,000 per year, and other sponsorship funds provided US$50,000 per year. The Community Action Plan is financed by the community using its own budget.

Strengths
Plan conducted a pilot project assessment and examined outcome data. The data showed strong and positive results. Plan also has a special and strong emphasis on inclusion for children with disabilities, the only program we know of to focus specifically on this population. Organizers require that group size stays small, which usually promotes intimacy and engagement among parents. There is a specific intention to include fathers. And Plan uses a unique approach that capitalizes on local wisdom and families' strengths, such that parents rely heavily on each other for problem solving and effective parenting skills.

Evaluation Data
- In 2014, 576 out of 613 parents (94 percent) interviewed reported applying skills learned at home (for example, brushing teeth, playing with children, using words of affirmation and positive discipline)Exclusive breastfeeding rates increased from 16 percent in 2010 to 48 percent in 2012
- 79 out of 85 parenting groups (93 percent) initiated Community Action Plans to benefit young children in the community

Recommendations
- Standardize the structure of parenting sessions. Currently, *kaders* decide on both the content and delivery of the service, which makes evaluation information difficult to interpret. A standardized structure, more specifically targeted and measured outcomes would strengthen evaluation information, and focusing groups on teachable moments or transition periods with specific populations in mind would strengthen outcomes.
- Schedule home visits. It is promising that home visits occur. However, the current practice of unannounced home visits seems logistically unsustainable; *kaders* do not know if parents will be at home and often have to make multiple visits to "catch" families at home.
- Create in-session practice time with children. Because Plan sessions already make room for full family participation in their Family Workshops, creating in-session practice time with children seems realistically feasible and was also recommended by external reviewers in an NTT pilot program analysis.
- Formalize partnerships with the government for sustainability.

Save the Children's Parenting Meetings

Overview
Save the Children is an international nongovernmental organization that promotes children's rights and tries to improve children's lives by improving services in education, health care, child protection, and emergency aid sectors.

Several Save the Children projects in Aceh and Nusa Tenggara Timur (NTT) in particular have a component that involves outreach to and engagement with parents, known as parenting meetings.

Location
Sessions are held at PAUD (ECD) centers, mainly in rural areas.

Content
- Once a month, usually lasting one to two hours. Minimum of five sessions per year. Typically held in the afternoon after school.
- Save the Children facilitators, who are called Master Trainers, present a prese-lected message to the group, may lead the group in games (particularly those that can be played with children at home), and provide time for discussion, questions and answers. Master Trainers expect ECD teachers in the PAUD to conduct complementary home visits.
- Every month Master Trainers meet before going into the field. Together they decide what the messages and materials should be and how to deliver them, as well as review the previous month's sessions. They each deliver the same message in the same month.
- Both fathers and mothers are invited, and normally fathers do come. Children do not attend the meetings—helpers watch the children during meetings. In addition to parents of children enrolled in PAUD, organizers also normally invite the head of the village and religious leaders.
- After five months (and five sessions), involvement of the Save the Children field office ends, but ideally the community continues to run the program independently, discussing early childhood related topics according to the needs of the parents.

Facilitators
Facilitators working directly with parents in the Save the Children approach are called Master Trainers. They are mostly ECD teachers while some are school supervisors, principals, and ECD directors. Master Trainers are the main facilita-tors of the meetings, but they also invite local experts when parents ask for additional information. In addition to facilitating the parent meetings and their "day job" as teachers or principals, Master Trainers also provide technical assis-tance or coaching to teachers. Master Trainers receive transportation reimburse-ment only, not a salary or incentive.

Coverage
Below is coverage information on specific Save the Children programs that include parenting meetings.

Financing
As an example, the parenting meetings in Malaka's SPECIAL program had an annual operating cost of Rp 45.4 million in 2013/14.

Box A.7   Program Coverage in Aceh and Nusa Tengarra Timur (NTT)

In Aceh, two programs are operating in the Bener Meriah district:

- *Better Living, Education, Nutrition and Development 3 (BLEND 3)*: targets 1,000 parents/caregivers in 41 *posyandu* and/or 46 preschools
- *Basic Initiative for School Access (BISA)*: targets 200 parents/caregivers in 15 ECD centers.

In NTT, three programs are operating in West Sumba, Atambua, and the Malaka district:

- *Safe and Positive Education for Children in Indonesia with Active Learning (SPECIAL)*: targets 1,500 parents/caregivers
- *Better Literacy for Academic Results (BELAJAR)*: Unavailable
- *Strengthening Education through Awareness and Reading Achievement (SETARA)*: targets 800 parents at 40 ECD centers.

Strengths

Save the Children's parenting meetings are highly localized—and may be the only program proactively addressing the complicated issue of local languages— aims to meet families' needs in poor and rural areas, and has small, interactive group sessions. It focuses on families' knowledge and strengths and makes apt use of local resources and materials. It also addresses the important issue of inclusion for children with special needs. Organizers have put in place strong training and support mechanisms, relative to some other programs. Master Trainers get initial training but also meet monthly thereafter to review progress and challenges and problem solve.

The program serves families whose children are already enrolled in a PAUD program. This allows for the integration and continuity of messages between early childhood programs and parenting programs, which benefits children and parents. It also allows an opportunity for in-session practice of new skills with children, observations, and feedback, as long as sessions are held with some overlap during the day.

Recommendations

- Content of the sessions could be strengthened by focusing on children's emotional development and communication and by helping parents learn positive discipline techniques
- Program could be strengthened by naming and measuring specific parenting education outcomes for both parents and children and evaluating results at the national level.

Box A.8   Evaluations and Plans for the Future

At the end of each month, master trainers meet to evaluate how activities went during the month. The discussion centers not only on how parent meetings went, but also on how "cluster meetings" went (district-organized professional development meetings for ECD teachers, which Save the Children works to strengthen in its areas), and any miscellaneous activities that might have occurred during the month, such as a children's performance. During the meeting, they discuss challenges and how to address them in the coming month, as well as parent responses.

Country office staff's anecdotal observations suggest that as a result of parent meetings, parents tend to bring their children to PAUD centers on a more regular basis, become more involved in the center, and spontaneously look for ways to show support to the program (for example, bringing fans from home without being asked). They also tend to make toys or bring their own ideas or materials from home to share with the program.

To strengthen capacity in all areas, staff will likely implement a "cross-monitoring" system wherein staff from NTT visits the Aceh field offices to provide guidance and support, especially since both working areas cover rural environments. They also plan to strengthen some services for infants and toddlers, namely regarding feeding practices. Overall, staff views their support for the regular parent meetings as a key strategy to improving capacity in local areas to increase children's health and well-being.

World Vision International

Overview

World Vision is a faith-based, nongovernmental, nonprofit organization that promotes a Christian philosophy while working to improve the lives of children of any background. World Vision has 51 local offices in Indonesia, all located in poor communities, of which 8 have early childhood education components. Two sites (Poso in Sulawesi and Alor-Sikka in Nusa Tengarra Timur) currently have parenting education components. They can be in the form of individual counseling on feeding practices or in group meetings.

Location

Families receive parenting education from World Vision at *posyandu* (village health posts), PAUD, a parent's home, church, or community center.

Content

For individual counseling on feeding practices:

- Families visit *posyandu* on a given day and after registration, rotate through five "centers" at the clinic. At the fourth table, they receive parenting education via consultation. The individual counseling provides a chance to both receive information and ask questions on feeding practices.

For group meetings:

- Typically meets once per month for two hours. Groups decide for themselves on the timing, frequency, and duration of meetings.
- The meetings cover a mix of topics based on the needs of the whole child: health-related issues; children's needs for affection, play, and stimulation; promoting cognitive and academic progress; and child protection concerns. Groups and facilitators select topics as they have interest and as they address the goals the community has named. They may combine or skip topics as they see fit.
- The guidelines for each topic exist in a manual for facilitators. For each module, the manual provides a four-page set of information for facilitators that provides session objectives, simple activity suggestions and basic background reading materials to inform facilitators.

Facilitators

World Vision Indonesia's local office staff (area development program staff members) and *posyandu kaders* may facilitate parenting education meetings but they rely heavily on specialists to lead meetings relevant to their field. A bidding process involving at least three bidders allows staff to choose the best person to facilitate the meetings. A coordination meeting between staff and the consultant takes place before implementation to ensure the messages are clear and agreed on, per the World Vision International guidelines. Area development program staff members receive a salary from the national office. Other consultants and facilitators may or may not be paid; that decision is determined locally.

Coverage

Data unavailable.

Financing

As an example, one of World Vision's home-based early childhood education programs in Alor—which includes parenting education—had an annual operating budget of Rp 60 million.

Strengths

The materials for facilitators are very strong. The breadth of topics covering children's holistic needs is excellent, and the design of the materials seems easy to digest and is visually appealing. Facilitators receive about four pages of information on each topic, with session objectives, activities, and background reading clearly laid out. These materials could conceivably be a model for other programs to emulate.

Recommendation

Implement a standardized evaluation. At present, activities and evaluations are entirely localized. As a result, there is no systematic information at the national-level about key components of the sessions, such as how frequently they meet, how many parents attend, what outcomes are desired and achieved, and who delivers the information well.

Note

1. At the time of publication in March 2015, plans to implement the MoEC grant program for children ages zero to three had been canceled.

Bibliography

AFC (Administration for Children and Families). 2002. *Making a Difference in the Lives of Infants and Toddlers and Their Families: The Impacts of Early Head Start.* Washington, DC: US Department of Health and Human Services.

Agarwal-Harding, S., H. Alatas, T. Pakasi, and Gutama. 2014. *Early Childhood Care and Development: Plan's Parenting Education Program in Indonesia, An Assessment Pilot Phase in Nusa Tengarra Timur.* Jakarta: Plan International Indonesia.

Andina, S., and H. B. Tomlinson. 2013. *PKH Education Team Field Visit Report from Yogyakarta and North Sulawesi.* Poverty Reduction and Economic Management Sector. Jakarta, Indonesia: World Bank.

Arthur, W. J., W. J. Bennett, P. Stanush, and T. L. McNelly. 1998. "Factors That Influence Skill Decay and Retention: A Quantitative Review and Analysis." *Human Performance* 11: 57–101.

Barlow, J., I. Johnston, D. Kendrick, L. Polnay, and S. Stewart-Brown. 2006. "Individual and Group-Based Parenting Programmes for the Treatment of Physical Child Abuse and Neglect." *Cochrane Database of Systemic Reviews* 3: 1–20.

Black, M., P. Nair, C. Kight, R. Wachtel, P. Roby, and M. Schuler. 1994. "Parenting and Early Development among Children of Drug-Abusing Women: Effects of Home Intervention." *Pediatrics* 94: 440–48.

Brooks-Gunn, J., and L. B. Markman. 2005. "The Contribution of Parenting to Ethnic and Racial Gaps in School Readiness." *The Future of Children* 15 (1): 139–68.

Brooks-Gunn, J., L. Berlin, and A. S. Fuligni. 2000. "Early Childhood Intervention Programs: What about the Family?" In *Handbook of Early Childhood Intervention*, 2nd ed., edited by J. P. Shonkoff, and S. J. Meisel. New York: Cambridge University Press.

Brooks-Gunn, J., C. McCarton, P. Casey, M. McCormick, C. Bauer, J. Bernbaum, et al. 1994. "Early Intervention in Low Birth Weight, Premature Infants: Results through Age 5 Years from the Infant Health and Development Program." *Journal of the American Medical Association* 272 (16): 1257–62.

Bugental, B., and A. Schwartz. 2009. "A Cognitive Approach to Child Mistreatment Prevention among Medically At-Risk Infants." *Developmental Psychology* 45: 284–88.

Cahyono, W., M. Estrely, A. Chandra, and D. Chrisnatalia. 2010. *Situational Analysis on ECCD Program.* Facultas Psikolgi Universitas Indonesia, Pusat Krisis. Jakarta: PLAN Indonesia.

CDC (Centers for Disease Control and Prevention). 2009. *Parent Training Programs: Insight for Practitioners.* Atlanta: U.S. Department of Health and Human Services, Centers for Disease Control and Prevention.

Chilman, C. S. 1973. "Programs for Disadvantaged Parents." In *Review of Child Development Research*, Vol. 3, edited by B. M. Caldwell and H. N. Ricciuti, 403–65. Chicago: University of Chicago Press.

Chao, R., and V. Tseng. 2002. "Parenting of Asians." In *Handbook of Parenting: Vol. 4. Social Conditions and Applied Parenting*. 2nd ed., edited by M. H. Bornstein, 59–93. Mahwah, NJ: Erlbaum.

Colosi, L., and R. Dunifon. 2003. *Effective Parent Education Programs*. Ithaca, NY: Cornell Cooperative Extension.

Cooper, P. J., M. Landman, M. Tomlinson, C. Molteno, L. Swartz, and L. Murray. 2002. "Impact of a Mother-infant Intervention in an Indigent Peri-urban South African Context: Pilot Study." *British Journal of Psychiatry* 180: 76–81.

Duggan, A., E. McFarlane, A. Windham, C. Rohde, D. Salkever, L. Fuddy, et al. 1999. "Evaluation of Hawaii's Healthy Start Program." *The Future of Children* 9: 66–90.

Eshel, N., B. Daelmans, M. C. de Mello, and J. Martines. 2006. "Responsive Parenting: Interventions and Outcomes." *Bulletin of the World Health Organization* 84 (12): 992–99.

Evans, J. 2006. *Parenting Programmes: An Important ECD Intervention Strategy*. Paris: UNESCO.

Gardner, J. M., S. P. Walker, C. A. Powell, and S. Grantham-McGregor. 2003. "A Randomized Controlled Trial of a Home-visiting Intervention on Cognition and Behavior in Term Low Birth Weight Infants." *Journal of Pediatrics* 143: 634–39.

Gelfand, D., D. Teti, S. Seiner, and P. Jameson. 1996. "Helping Mothers Fight Depression: Evalutaion of a Home-based Intervention Progrma for Depressed Mothers and Their Infants." *Journal of Clinical Child Psychology* 25: 406–22.

Grindal, T., J. Bowne, H. Yoshikawa, G. Duncan, K. Magnuson, and H. Schindler. 2013. *The Added Impact of Parenting Education in Early Childhood Education Programs: A Meta-Analysis*. Manuscript under review.

Hasan, A., M. Hyson, and M. Chang, eds. 2013. *Early Childhood Education and Development in Poor Villages of Indonesia: Strong Foundations, Later Success*. Washington, DC: World Bank.

Heinicke, C., N. Fineman, V. Ponce, and D. Guthrie. 2001. "Relation-based Intervention with At-risk Mothers: Outcome in the Second Year of Life." *Infant Mental Health Journal* 22 (4): 431–62.

Heinicke, C., N. Fineman, C. Rodning, G. Ruth, S. Recchia, and D. Guthrie. 1999. "Relationship-Based Intervention with At-risk Mothers: Outcome in First Year of Life." *Infant Mental Health Journal* 20: 349–74.

Hoff-Ginsberg, E., and T. Tardiff. 1995. "Socioeconomic Status and Parenting." In *Handbook of Parenting: Vol. 2. Biology and Ecology of Parenting*, edited by M. H. Bornstein, 161–188. Mahwah, NJ: Erlbaum.

Howrigan, G. A. 1988. "Fertility, Infant Feeding, and Change in Yucatan." In *Parental Behavior in Diverse Societies*, edited by R. A. LeVine, P. M. Miller, and M. M. West, 3–12. San Francisco: Jossey-Bass.

Huser, M., S. A. Small, and G. Eastman. 2008. *What Research Tells Us about Effective Parenting Education Programs*. Madison, WI: University of Wisconsin-Madison/ Extension.

Hyson, M., and H. B. Tomlinson. 2014. *The Early Years Matter: Education, Care, and the Well-Being of Children, Birth to 8*. New York: Teachers College Press.

Jacobson, S., and K. Frye. 1991. "Effect of Maternal Social Support on Attachment: Experimental Evidence." *Child Development* 62 (3): 572–82.

Johnson, Z., F. Howell, and B. Molloy. 1993. "Community Mothers' Programme: Randomised Controlled Trial on Non-professional Intervention in Parenting." *British Medical Journal* 306: 1449–52.

Joyce, B., and B. Showers. 2002. *Student Achievement though Staff Development.* Alexandria, VA: Association for Supervision and Curriculum Development.

Kitzman, H., R. Cole, H. Yoos, and D. Olds. 1997. "Challenges Experienced by Home Visitors: A Qualitative Study of Program Implementation." *Journal of Community Psychology* 25 (1): 95–109.

Knerr, W., F. Gardner, and L. Cluver. 2013. "Improving Positive Parenting Skills and Reducing Harsh and Abusive Parenting in Low- and Middle-income Countries: A Systematic Review." *Prevention Science* 14 (4): 352–63.

Kumpfer, K. K. 1999. *Strengthening America's Families: Exemplary Parenting and Family Strategies for Delinquency Prevention.* Washington, DC: U.S. Office of Juvenile Justice and Delinquency Prevention.

Landry, S. H., K. E. Smith, P. R. Swank, T. Zucker, A. D. Crawford, and E. F. Solari. 2012. "The Effects of a Responsive Parenting Intervention on Parent-Child Interactions during Shared Book Reading." *Developmental Psychology* 48 (4): 969–86.

Lee, E., S. Mitchell-Herzfeld, A. Lowensfels, R. Greene, V. Dorabawila, and K. DuMont. 2009. "Reducing Low Birth Weight through Home Visitation: A Randomized Controlled Trial." *American Journal of Preventative Medicine* 36: 154–60.

Love, J., E. E. Kisker, C. Ross, H. Raikes, J. Constaine, K. Boller, et al. 2005. "The Effectiveness of Early Head Start for 3-Year-Old Children and Their Parents." *Developmental Psychology* 41: 885–901.

Lundahl, B., H. Risser, and M. Lovejoy. 2006. "A Meta-analysis of Parent Training: Moderators and Follow-up Effects." *Clinical Psychology Review* 26: 86–104.

Malhomes, V., and R. King, eds.2012. *The Oxford Handbook of Poverty and Child Development.* New York: Oxford University Press.

Myers, R. G., and R. Hertenberg. 1987. *The Eleven Who Survive: Toward a Re-examination of Early Childhood Development Program Options and Costs.* New York: Consultative Group on Early Childhood Care and Education, UNICEF.

Olds, D., J. Robinson, L. Pettitt, D. Luckey, J. Holmberg, R. Ng, et al. 2004. "Effects of Home Visits by Paraprofessionals and by Nurses: Age-four Follow-up of a Randomized Trial." *Pediatrics* 114: 1560–68.

President of the Republic of Indonesia. 2013. *Regulation of the President of the Republic of Indonesia Number 60 Year 2013 about Integrated Holistic Early Childhood Development.* Jakarta: Cabinet Secretariat RI.

Reed, C. J. 2013. "Indonesia—The World's Most Social Mobile Centric Country." May 9 Retrieved from The Wall: http://wallblog.co.uk/2013/05/09/indonesia-the-worlds-most-social-mobile-centric-country/.

Reese, E., A. Sparks, and D. Leyva. 2010. "A Review of Parent Interventions for Preschool Children's Language and Emergent Literacy." *Journal of Early Childhood Literacy* 10 (1): 97–117.

Salas, E., and J. Cannon-Bowers. 2001. "The Science of Training: A Decade of Progress." *Annual Review of Psychology* 52: 471–99.

Super, C. M., M. G. Herrera, and J. O. Mora. 1990. "Long-term Effects of Food Supplementation and Psychosocial Intervention on the Physical Growth of Colombian Infants at Risk of Malnutrition." *Child Development* 61: 29–49.

Turner, H., C. Nye, and J. Schwartz. 2004/2005. "Assessing the Effects of Parent Involvement Interventions on Elementary School Student Achievement." *The Evaluation Exchange* X (4): 1–24.

Van den Boom, D. 1995. "Do First Year Intervention Effects Endure? Follow-up during Toddlerhood of a Sample of Dutch Irritable Infants." *Child Development* 66 (6), 1798–816.

Walker, S. P., S. M. Change, C. A. Powell, and S. M. Grantham-McGregor. 2004. "Psychosocial Intervention Improves the Development of Low-birth-weight Infants." *Journal of Nutrition 134*: 1417–23.

Wasik, B. H., and D. Bryant. 2009. *Essentials of Funding Home Visiting Programs: Hiring, Training, and Supervising Home Visitors*. Washington, DC: Society for Research on Child Development.

Webster-Stratton, C., and J. Reid. 2010. "Adapting the Incredible Years, an Evidence-based Parenting Programme, for Families Involved in the Child Welfare System." *Journal of Children's Services* 5: 25–42.

Whitebook, M., and A. Eichberg. (n.d.). *Finding a Better Way: Defining and Assessing Public Policies to Improve Child Care Workforce Compensation*. Berkeley, CA: Center for the Study of Child Care Employment.

World Bank. (2012). *PKH Conditional Cash Transfer: Social Assistance Program and Public Expenditure Review 6*. Jakarta: World Bank.

The World Bank, COMMGAP. (n.d.). *Theories of Behavior Change*. Communication for Governance and Accountability Program. Washington, DC: The World Bank.

World Vision. (2013). *Summary Report on Child Well Being: World Vision Indonesia's Contribution to Child Well Being FY 2012*. Jakarta: World Vision Indonesia.

Zubrick, S., G. Smith, J. Nicholson, A. Sanson, T. Jackiewicz, and the LSAC Consortium. 2008. "Parenting and Families in Australia." Social Policy Research Paper No. 34, Canberra, Australia: FaHCSIA (Department of Families, Housing, Community Services and Indigenous Affairs).

Environmental Benefits Statement

The World Bank Group is committed to reducing its environmental footprint. In support of this commitment, the Publishing and Knowledge Division leverages electronic publishing options and print-on-demand technology, which is located in regional hubs worldwide. Together, these initiatives enable print runs to be lowered and shipping distances decreased, resulting in reduced paper consumption, chemical use, greenhouse gas emissions, and waste.

The Publishing and Knowledge Division follows the recommended standards for paper use set by the Green Press Initiative. The majority of our books are printed on Forest Stewardship Council–certified paper, with nearly all containing 50–100 percent recycled content. The recycled fiber in our book paper is either unbleached or bleached using Totally Chlorine Free (TCF), Processed Chlorine Free (PCF), or Enhanced Elemental Chlorine Free (EECF) processes.

More information about the Bank's environmental philosophy can be found at http://crinfo.worldbank.org/wbcrinfo/node/4.

green press
INITIATIVE

www.ingramcontent.com/pod-product-compliance
Lightning Source LLC
Chambersburg PA
CBHW080001280326
41935CB00013B/1710